PARTNERING FOR SUCCESS:

STRATEGIES FOR EFFECTIVE PARENT-TEACHER CONFERENCES

Tricia Shelton, EdD

Gryphon House, Inc.
www.gryphonhouse.com

Published by Gryphon House, Inc.
P. O. Box 10, Lewisville, NC 27023

800.638.0928; 877.638.7576 [fax]

Visit us on the web at www.gryphonhouse.com.

Library of Congress Control Number: 2024952078

BULK PURCHASE
Gryphon House books are available for special premiums and sales promotions as well as for fund-raising use. Special editions or book excerpts can also be created to specifications. For details, call 800.638.0928.

Table of Contents

Introduction

I am really looking forward to my child's next school conference!

—FUTURE CLASSROOM PARENT OF THE TEACHER READING THIS BOOK

Family-teacher conferences are a conventional aspect of the school year calendar. Whether students are part of traditional public, private, charter, or cyber schools, conferences between teachers and families are a usual occurrence in many classrooms. Moreover, conferences have long been a staple in schools, creating familiarity around the event for many stakeholders. Truly, conferences are an anticipated rite of passage for families and are as expected in early childhood classrooms as play centers and picture books.

Despite their experience with school conferencing, families may feel uneasy about the whole process. When expectations for communication are unclear, families may be confused about their role. Prior negative school encounters as a student, parent, or both can shape the outlook that families bring with them to conferences as well. From these previous interactions with teachers and other school leadership, some families learn passive or defensive conference behaviors that hinder them from fully participating in discussions.

Conference expectations can feel unclear for teachers, too. While most educators value interaction with families, teachers often have little direct instruction on how to lead effective conferences. Without reflecting on their skills, teachers will fail to engage families effectively and minimize their own professional confidence in the process. Consequently, conferencing becomes a worrisome and overwhelming event for teachers.

A lack of adequate professional development resources compounds this issue. Courses centered solely on family-teacher conferencing are rare in teacher preparation programs. Further, many reliable publications embed discussions about school conferencing within family engagement practices rather than exploring its benefits as an independent strategy. This book was written to address those gaps in conference knowledge for teachers.

HOW TO USE THIS BOOK

Early childhood is the "prime time" for establishing strong relationships with families. Conferences capitalize on these positive relationships to support children's holistic development. This book offers ways to prepare for productive conversations with families throughout the conference process. Each chapter highlights specific strategies for positive interaction before, during, and after family conferencing.

Before reading, teachers might reflect on their conferencing strengths and needs and use those insights to inform their reading focus. As they read, early childhood educators are encouraged to note similarities between the vignettes and anecdotes in each chapter and their own interactions with students and families. These examples are included to prompt perspective sharing and critical thinking while supplying the motivation to improve conference skill sets.

Chapter 1: Understanding the Family-Teacher Conference, explores the benefits of effective communication between family members and teachers and outlines a strong framework for developing the conference's purpose. Further, readers will learn how a supportive classroom culture can set the foundation for productive conferencing.

Chapter 2: Planning for Success discusses how teachers can use the conference purpose to define goals for family-teacher collaboration and make intentional plans for collaboration through supporting family needs. Teachers will also learn how a positive mindset can develop and sustain a collaborative tone for conferencing.

Chapter 3: Creating a Welcoming Environment builds on the benefits of a positive conference tone by prompting teachers to reflect on their efforts to create a welcoming environment for all families. In doing so, teachers will be asked to think about their biases and consider how they can engage in perspective-sharing with families. This chapter also offers recommendations for working with linguistically diverse families.

Chapter 4: Active Listening and Effective Communication looks at how active listening and effective communication enhance and advance all conference strategies. The chapter discusses the strengths and weaknesses of individual communication styles and the challenges to effective communication, along with methods for overcoming these barriers.

Chapter 5: Collecting Appropriate Documentation highlights the importance of student documentation as a means of supporting family-teacher communication efforts. Teachers will find descriptions of a variety of documentation and descriptions of the distinctive benefits of each type. Teachers will also learn ways to invite families to share their own student documentation from the home setting.

Chapter 6: Partnering for Problem Solving addresses the importance of strong documentation and communication to facilitate effective problem solving in the conference setting. This chapter looks at some of the most prominent student concerns and offers recommendations for how teachers and families can work together to navigate student challenges.

Chapter 7: Celebrating Achievements shares ideas for positive messaging to communicate student growth and encourage ongoing progress. Recognizing student successes can be motivating for students and their families.

Chapter 8: Following Up and Following Through puts all the pieces of effective conferencing together to develop and implement viable action planning for student success. This section provides teachers with direction for useful reflection on the conference process from the first minutes to weeks after the school meeting.

This book offers teachers useful planning tools to promote meaningful discussion and active engagement from all stakeholders. These planning tools are designed to meet specific teacher needs; therefore, each conference tool may not be appropriate for every educator. Likewise, the structured guidance the planning tools provide may not be essential for every family-teacher conference. Instead, teachers should reflect on their professional conferencing skills and use the tools that they believe will best enhance their interaction and engagement with individual families. The resources in the reference section offer additional guidance on topics raised in this book as well as supplemental readings and electronic sources.

A WORD ON FAMILY DIVERSITY

Successful children often have a support network composed of extended family, guardians, and community members. In this text, the terms *parent* and *family* are used interchangeably as inclusive terms to refer to all caring adults who assume a participatory role in school conferencing, educational decision-making, and/or supportive practices in the home. The use of these terms that signify biological relationships between children and adults is not meant to devalue or disregard other types of guardianship. Instead, the language choice is made to acknowledge and honor the diverse cultural structures that define *family* for young children.

Strengths and expertise represent another critical area of difference among families. To lead productive conferences, teachers must employ some family-specific strategies. As such, this book will also discuss how teachers can use school conferencing to build positive relationships with families. Strong connections with families create comfort and security, garnering a sense of trust that teachers can apply to the conference setting.

FROM THE MOUTHS OF FAMILIES

While this book offers strategies to support teacher conferencing skills, it also considers the value of effective conferencing from the family perspective. Each chapter begins with a quote from a family navigating the conference process. Their words of frustration and gratitude remind teachers of the significant effects that school conferences have on shaping family attitudes toward teachers and school.

Yet, unlike the other family quotes that introduce the following chapters, the words at the opening of this introduction have not yet been spoken. This imagined quote is meant to motivate teachers. An effective conference gives hope to families and teachers alike. It is an opportunity to recognize collaborative efforts among students, families, and teachers. It is also a time to reinvest in family relationships to sustain progress over time. Given these positive outcomes, as the fictional quote suggests, both teachers and families have every reason to look forward to conferences with enthusiasm and anticipation.

CHAPTER 1

UNDERSTANDING THE FAMILY-TEACHER CONFERENCE

A good conference meeting always makes me feel a little better about sending my child to school.

—PARENT OF A KINDERGARTEN STUDENT

Families are a vital part of student success in the classroom. Although teachers are responsible for preparing and implementing instruction, families take the lead in instilling the importance of education in their children. Further, families who value education are more likely to assume an active role in monitoring their child's academic growth and social development. They reinforce learning expectations and provide appropriate support in the home setting. With this level of encouragement, students grow to appreciate their strengths, cultivating a lifetime of enthusiasm for learning.

Recognizing the influence of family engagement in the classroom, many teachers offer a variety of opportunities for families to participate in their children's learning. The most common in early childhood classrooms are volunteer experiences and family events. In both cases, these sessions require in-person participation, inviting families to visit the school setting. More recently, however, COVID-19 protocols prompted educators to explore virtual engagement options. Remote broadcasting and virtual conferencing have provided viable engagement alternatives for families with limited flexibility in their schedules and/or transportation needs.

Nonetheless, family engagement in all its forms is always centered on establishing open communication between school and home. From attending a school play to chaperoning a zoo field trip to donating a box of tissues, family engagement cultivates positive relationship building between teachers and families. Both groups learn more about each other, establishing a strong foundation for collaboration. Additionally, as families become involved in the classroom community, they learn more about school expectations, instructional goals, and their child's progress. Armed with this knowledge, families are better prepared to support the child's developmental growth.

A family-teacher conference is a quintessential example of school communication. These meetings are a longstanding tradition in most schools, viewed as a significant milestone in a student's academic year. In response to school efforts to partner with families more fully, the nature of these conferences has evolved. Gone are the days of teachers summoning families for a lecture on student performance, followed by a critique of their parenting choices. Instead, today's teachers should expect to learn as much as they impart during their conferences.

The quote at the beginning of this chapter reminds teachers of all that hangs in the balance of a well-executed family-teacher conference. For some families, the conference setting is their initial encounter with their child's school environment. It is the teacher's opportunity to offer a strong first impression. A meeting featuring open communication, perspective-sharing, and genuine responsiveness can go a long way toward building and sustaining trust between teachers and families. As such, it's important for teachers to acknowledge the ability of these conferences to solidify successful outcomes for students and their families.

Benefits of the Family-Teacher Conference

At its most basic level, a family-teacher conference is a conversation. School conferencing should bring together teachers and families in a way that encourages conversation about a student's progress in school. Family-teacher conferences are meant to offer all parties a chance to assume the role of speaker and listener to build understanding. Much like other types of conversation, the family-teacher conference has its ups and downs that can make participants—families and teachers—feel happy, sad, frustrated, or content.

Despite the range of emotions they may evoke, family-teacher conferences offer many benefits for students, families, and teachers. Most importantly, the collaborative discussion that happens during school conferences highlights student strengths and challenges. With this information, teachers can better tailor learning activities to meet student needs, yielding greater achievement over time.

When students are a part of effective family-teacher conferences, they have strong models of cooperative interaction and problem solving. A preschool child who sees her father and teacher taking turns speaking learns she can be heard without tantrums or yelling. A kindergartener who watches his grandmother and teacher use polite words in their conversation recognizes the value of showing respect to others. Similarly, the second-grade student who is invited to share insight about his low test scores in reading begins to accept accountability in his learning. In all these examples, students receive greater consistency in social-skill development across home and school settings.

Families, too, gain from successful conference experiences. Productive communication with teachers can send a powerful message to families that they are significant contributors to their children's education. These feelings can boost family confidence, encouraging families to take a more active role in setting goals and making decisions for their children. Additionally, positive conferencing can affect how families view and value school. To families who may be reluctant to trust school systems, a positive family-teacher conference can reshape their perception of school in a constructive way.

For teachers, effective conferencing builds important skills that enhance their professional repertoire. Working with a wide variety of families helps teachers hone their communication skills. Teachers who are highly skilled in listening and speaking are better able to establish positive relationships with students and their families. When families trust teachers, they are more likely to share insight that deepens the teacher's awareness of the child and the family. Such child-specific information can affect academic progress, student behavior, and social development.

WHAT IS CULTURAL HUMILITY?

In 1998, Melanie Tervalon and Jann Murray-Garcia named cultural humility as a crucial disposition of community professionals. In education, cultural humility develops sensitivity and awareness of diverse perspectives, encouraging inclusive practices within schools.

The underlying belief of cultural humility is that individuals cannot "master" cultural understanding. Instead, it is a lifelong process that requires consistent and committed effort. In pursuing cultural humility, Tervalon and Murray-Garcia outline three core principles:

- challenges to power imbalances,
- community partnerships, and
- self-critique.

The conference setting offers many opportunities to explore the elements of cultural humility. By learning from diverse family structures, parenting strategies, and family traditions, teachers can begin to examine their biases and build stronger relationships with families. They learn to share their power with families to make decisions in the best interest of students. Similarly, cultural humility promotes advocacy around family and community needs, which benefits every stakeholder in the school environment.

Setting the Framework for a Successful Conference

When implemented properly, the family-teacher conference can build an effective partnership between families and teachers. A strong framework creates alignment between the conference's purpose and outcomes, holding teachers accountable to evidence-based family engagement practices. However, the best frameworks for school partnerships solicit and value the contributions of teachers and families equally, providing each stakeholder with a voice in conference goals.

Joyce Epstein and colleagues (2019) designed a reputable and proven approach to establishing family engagement, the "Framework of Six Types of Involvement for Comprehensive Programs of Partnership and Sample Practices". Although the framework offers guidance on multiple areas of family involvement, the structure provides practical recommendations for centering the conference. Epstein and her colleagues suggest the following types of family involvement that also can serve as the focus of family-teaching conferencing:

- **Parenting:** The conference discussion addresses how families can support school success through parenting choices and guidance.
- **Communication:** Teachers and families use the conference to determine effective means of communicating with each other during the school year.
- **Volunteering:** Within the conference, families explore opportunities to support the learning community through volunteer experiences at the school.
- **Learning at home:** Given student needs, teachers and families explore home learning options to reinforce student progress.
- **Decision-making:** Through discussion, families advocate for appropriate supports and programming for their children.
- **Collaborating with community:** Teachers and families investigate how community services and resources can support students in the classroom.

Each of these types of family involvement directly affects student achievement. Early childhood teachers may be quick to note that these practices invest in the whole child rather than solely academic performance. Both individually and collectively, these student supports motivate families to take an active role in their child's education. This is why teachers should attempt to integrate each of these engagement practices in every conference discussion. See the following table for sample topics for each of the six types of family involvement.

Family Involvement Type	Sample Conference Discussion Topics
PARENTING	• Recommendations for reading with children • Toilet training tips • Suggestions for homework stations in the home
COMMUNICATION	• Uses for a home-school journal • Curriculum materials and resources • Review of daily classroom schedule
VOLUNTEERING	• Explanation of classroom needs, such as field trip chaperone, teacher helper, and so on • Fundraising support for school activities • Solicitation of family input via focus groups or surveys
LEARNING AT HOME	• Explanation of student progress • Review of testing results • Discussion of student evaluation protocols
DECISION-MAKING	• Suggestions for family-child activities that prompt naturalistic learning, such as building with blocks, cooking, crafting, and so on • Ideas for supporting social-skill development in the home • Coupling of behavior rewards and consequences across home and school
COLLABORATING WITH THE COMMUNITY	• Available resources for families within the school community • Community service opportunities • Family support/advocacy groups

Conference Purpose

Several events can trigger a conference between teachers and families. For instance, prior communication with a family member may necessitate a lengthier, in-person discussion. An incident or behavior in the classroom could inspire a conference as well. Other conferences are planned simply as regular communication during the school year. Regardless, every conference should have a dedicated purpose.

State the reason for the gathering so the discussion can be directed appropriately. In this way, the meeting is a good use of time for teachers and families. When a conference's purpose is unclear, communication is muddled, and neither group has an opportunity to examine their concerns fully or to explore potential resolutions. Misunderstandings often follow, intensifying student challenges. Very often, these conference barriers lead to feelings of frustration and indifference.

Teachers and families should agree on the conference's purpose before setting a meeting date. Some conference purposes will be highly specialized, aligning with the unique concerns of the teacher, child, or family. By being upfront with any significant issues, teachers and families can plan well for effective engagement. Naming the conference purpose allows each group to reflect on the child's strengths and needs to offer thoughtful insight and understanding to the conversation. Common themes for conference purposes include the following:

- **Developmental expectations:** To gauge student progress properly, families should be aware of expected growth in each developmental domain. Advanced or restricted skill levels may require enrichment or remediation.
- **Academic progress:** Examining student growth in major academic areas informs goal setting for school and home alike.
- **Assessment data:** Teachers collect a variety of formal and informal data. Testing results can provide an objective perspective of student strengths and needs.
- **Behavioral concerns:** At times, teachers and families need to address student behaviors that may be hindering the child's success in the classroom or posing a safety concern to the child or their peers.

- **Social-emotional growth:** Because schools are shared spaces, social-emotional skills are tremendously important. Teachers should monitor progress and keep families abreast of significant changes in social conduct.
- **Resource sharing:** Teachers support students and their families through resource sharing. Providing students with helpful resources and connecting them with community groups can improve families' knowledge and skills.
- **Relationship building:** School conferencing provides an opportunity for families and teachers to become better acquainted with each other. Conferences centered on relationship building foster a foundation for trusting collaborative partnerships.

Conferences as Part of Classroom Culture

The culture of a classroom is shaped by many factors, including the classroom environment, curriculum, and instructional materials. But it is the people in the classroom—students, families, teachers, and other school leaders—who are most influential in shaping the culture of the classroom. The background of students and their families affects the classroom dynamics (see chapter 3, Creating a Welcoming Environment). Additionally, an educator's teaching and learning philosophy influences engagement practices tremendously.

How a teacher chooses to plan and lead family-teacher conferencing is representative of the classroom culture, too. Conferences that are centered on family participation enhance the school-home relationship. When teachers appreciate families and recognize their contributions to school success, they extend a sense of belonging within the classroom to families. Similarly, these sessions build important skill sets in both teachers and families that increase student progress and achievement. In this way, all members of the learning community thrive in their competencies.

It is not enough for teachers simply to want to hold successful conferences. A conference that is aligned with a positive classroom culture begins with how teachers view and understand the role of families in the success of their students. As members of the surrounding community themselves, teachers must be aware of the demographics of the school setting and offer appropriate accommodations to families. Yet teachers must see families individually, learning their strengths and needs. Lastly, to improve programming, teachers must be open to family input and be willing to see others' perspectives.

HONORING FAMILY FUNDS OF KNOWLEDGE

When teachers have differing experiences than their school families, they may see alternative outlooks or opinions as deficient. Teachers may also lump historically marginalized or linguistically diverse families into collective groups rather than exploring their individual characteristics. Such views create lower expectations for students and develop negative attitudes toward families among teachers. These biases can have a devastating effect on relationship building, prompting a disconnect between teachers and families.

A more productive approach deems families as unique but also special. The research of González, Moll, and Amanti (2005) recognized funds of knowledge as a means to creating effective family engagement in schools. The term *funds of knowledge* refers to the resources, expertise, and know-how that families collect as a result of their lived experiences. This diverse bank of intelligence works collectively to define family culture. Studying funds of knowledge fosters cross-cultural understanding in teachers that develops an awareness of individual family complexities.

Funds of knowledge can include a variety of talents. For instance, knowing how to play the piano, change a tire, speak Hebrew, or fry chicken are all examples of valuable funds of knowledge. Moreover, each of these competencies can serve as potential opportunities for growth for children. Through sharing these experiences with youth, families can develop children's academic, communicative, and social skills in profound and lasting ways.

Family-teacher conferencing can be an ideal time to discuss funds of knowledge. As teachers take time to get to know families, they gain insight into family resources. For example, during a conference, a parent may discuss the pastime of taking weekend camping trips with his four-year-old daughter. Reflecting on this information as a fund of knowledge, the teacher may identify how these family adventures could be an asset to the child's learning. Consider how the teacher might use this information to suggest ways to support mathematical readiness through authentic experiences at the campsite, such as counting the number of trees near their tent, comparing the lengths of sticks for the campfire, or estimating the number of marshmallows needed for the family s'mores. As teachers bond with families through their funds of knowledge, they strengthen the teacher-family relationship. Suggesting family-specific recommendations recognizes family interests and values, helping parents to feel heard and appreciated as individuals. Such a connection creates trust that can be useful when teachers and families need to discuss student challenges.

TIPS FOR DISCUSSING FAMILY FUNDS OF KNOWLEDGE

- Before the conference, conduct a home visit. Observe family interaction and behaviors that point to individual funds of knowledge. Encourage families to share more about their daily routines. Discuss ideas for incorporating these experiences in classroom learning for all students.
- Forward a questionnaire or survey to families about their interests and preferences. (See the *Family Questionnaire* on page 132.) Use the data to springboard conversation about the family's strengths.
- Solicit information about how families reinforce and support student learning in the home. In particular, celebrate any strategies that involve learning in daily activities, such as cooking, dancing, artwork, and so on.
- Take notes on what you learn about families from previous meetings or visits. Review this information before each conference. Consider how to use these experiences to enhance or support student learning in the home. Offer families specific example activity options.

How to Use the Family Questionnaire

The Family Questionnaire is a simple form for collecting data from families. While the questionnaire includes some basic questions, teachers may want to include other inquiries that may provide useful knowledge for their specific populations of students and/or families. Once revised appropriately, teachers can email the tool to families in advance of the first school conference. Another option is for teachers to distribute the tool for completion at school opening events, such as Open House or Back-to-School Night. Teachers may also follow up by telephone with families who do not return the form to collect their verbal responses.

Gathering information from families before the meeting helps teachers learn more about their students. It also provides some background on the strengths and needs of the family. During the conference, teachers can encourage families to elaborate on the insight shared in the questionnaire. Such conversations move beyond superficial small talk and deepen connections between teachers and families. Further, with this awareness, teachers can work with families to organize systems to support the child and to build a sense of investment in the school community as a whole.

Family-teacher conferences are a time-honored tradition in most contemporary schools. As many families cannot monitor their children's performance in the classroom daily, the conference serves as a dedicated opportunity for teachers and families to examine student progress. This means that teachers must be intentional about engaging families in the conference meeting. Referring to a structured conference framework ensures that educators explore a wide range of family engagement that builds and sustains strong family-teacher partnerships. Embedding these techniques in the classroom culture strengthens teacher commitment to individual family needs. Chapter 2 will explore how teachers can use this family-specific knowledge to develop goals for effective school conferencing.

FAMILY QUESTIONNAIRE

Welcome to our classroom! I am excited to work with you to make this a positive school year for your child. Please complete this questionnaire so that I can learn a little more about your family's interests, talents, and traditions.

Child's name:

Family member's name: **Relationship to the child:**

Family Information:

Who lives at home with the child? Please include names and relationships.

Does your family have any pets? If so, what kind?

Family Interests:

How does your family spend time together?

Briefly describe a recent or memorable family vacation or special outing.

Family Traditions:

What holidays/special days does your family celebrate?

What special traditions does your family have for these days?

Additional Information:

Is there anything else you would like to share about your family?

CHAPTER 2

PLANNING FOR SUCCESS

I know teachers have a lot of students, but my time is important too. Knowing there is a plan in place when I walk into a conference makes me feel valued as a parent.

—PARENT OF FIRST-GRADE TWINS

Teacher roles can be complex and overwhelming; this is especially true during conferencing time in the classroom. There are many tasks to address before, during, and after each family conference. These responsibilities become even more challenging when they are multiplied by the number of individual students within the classroom. Each child has unique strengths and needs, and without exception, teachers must be knowledgeable of these student qualities in every conference session.

Contemporary parents, too, are very busy people. Although many families recognize the significance of quality early childhood education, their work and home commitments can make it difficult to prioritize every school activity and obligation. Accordingly, when parents attend school meetings, teachers must make the most of their time with individual families. A family conference without specific direction is never in the best interest of teachers, parents, or students.

The parent quote at the beginning of this chapter reminds teachers of the deep connection between planning and positive family engagement. A well-planned conference sends a powerful message to families that the teacher respects their time as well as their expertise as thought partners. In this way, it is a significant first step toward opening the lines of communication between teachers and families, setting the foundation for professional, constructive relationship-building. Similarly, purposeful engagement practices to learn more about families, such as the Family Questionnaire on page 132, lay the foundation for positive home-school collaboration.

Conference planning is not just beneficial to families. Teachers who plan for conferences are often more prepared and confident to engage with families. Taking the time to identify major talking points helps teachers to anticipate potential conflicts in the conversation and to communicate ideas effectively. Through this process, teachers are better able to navigate any stumbling blocks that may arise during the conference.

After determining the purpose of the meeting, planning the conference design is the logical next step. Although the conference itself should be cooperative, the teacher, as the meeting initiator in most cases, should be responsible for developing a conference agenda. Of course, teachers should not expect families to be passive participants. Teachers must be intentional about setting a tone of purposeful family-teacher interaction.

Setting Family-Teacher Conference Goals

The goals of a parent-teacher conference are very different from the overall purpose. As discussed in the opening chapter, the purpose is the reason for holding the conference. It is the "why" that has brought the teacher and family together. Alternatively, the goals are the "how" the family and teacher will achieve the conference purpose. In most cases, the purpose will directly inform the conference goals.

Goal setting is crucial to successful conferencing. The typical conference schedule stacks meeting times with families one after another, which doesn't allow for last-minute planning and organization. Well-designed goals provide a focus for all attendees and ensure that the time together is used wisely. Further, conference goals hold both teachers and families accountable for contributing to the meeting. In short, conference goals ensure that both teachers and families can share their insights meaningfully.

Both the teacher and the family have expertise that the other lacks, so every conference should have teacher-directed goals and family-directed goals. As the name suggests, teacher expertise drives teacher-directed goals. Teachers use their professional knowledge and unique perspectives from within the classroom to share information with families. Teacher-directed goals may include discussing classroom behavioral concerns, test performance, or curriculum updates. By contrast, family-directed goals lean on the family's expertise in their child. Parents offer their specialized understanding of their children and the home environment to support the learning process. Family-directed goals may include sharing their child's interests, concerns, or family dreams.

There will certainly be some overlap among teacher- and family-directed goals. This intersection encourages useful discussion and collaboration. The following table provides some examples of teacher- and family-directed goals that could fall under the same conference purpose. In every case, the example goals for both teachers and family members would be enhanced with insight, questions, or ideas from their counterparts. For example, a teacher cannot partner with parents to support student progress if the family is unaware of grade-level curricular competencies. Similarly, a family would benefit little from sharing thoughts about a potential problem solution without listening to the teacher's thoughts about the practicality of its implementation in the classroom.

Four-year-old Gerald is a child who is working on building his independence in the classroom. Both his teacher and the family recognize this skill as critical for Gerald's transition to kindergarten. The teacher suggests encouraging Gerald to assume more personal responsibility in the classroom. As one suggestion, the teacher recommends that Gerald remove his outerwear on his own when he enters the classroom each morning and after outside play. The family appreciates this idea but knows that Gerald is easily frustrated when the zipper on his coat becomes stuck. The parent is concerned that Gerald's frustration could manifest itself as a tantrum.

As an initial alternative, the family requests that the teacher stand by Gerald to support him as he removes his coat and hat each day. In this way, Gerald has an opportunity to demonstrate independence, but the teacher can intervene quickly if he becomes overwhelmed. Although this plan seems reasonable, the teacher and the parent quickly realize that this approach conflicts with Gerald's classroom independence. Instead, the teacher and family work together to develop a plan to provide Gerald with some specific strategies to persist with challenges and to request help appropriately. The family agrees to encourage Gerald to use these same strategies in the home setting as well.

In this example, the teacher and family worked together to support the child. The teacher offered insight about age-appropriate adaptive skills and the family shared child-specific knowledge about the student's challenges. The teacher and family goals overlapped; both wanted the child to build independence, but the conference would have been far less productive without either perspective. With a clear purpose and by sharing their expert knowledge, the teacher and parent set and achieved practical goals at the conferencing meeting.

EXAMPLE CONFERENCE GOALS

Conference Purpose	Teacher-Directed Goals	Family-Directed Goals
TO SHARE CHILD'S PROGRESS IN LITERACY SKILLS	• Review recent formative assessment data. • Discuss curricular skills and competencies.	• Share family expectations for skill development. • Give examples of how the family supports literacy development in the home.
TO DEVELOP AN ACTION PLAN TO ADDRESS BITING BEHAVIOR	• Present anecdotal information about the observed biting behavior. • Discuss and revise current intervention practices.	• Recommend appropriate reinforcement for prosocial behaviors. • Explore possible motivators for the biting behaviors.
TO IMPROVE FINE MOTOR SKILLS	• Highlight developmental expectations with respect to academic skills, such as writing/drawing; adaptive skills, such as feeding; and play skills, such as dressing a doll. • Provide documentation of student strengths and needs in each of these skill areas.	• Offer feedback on current classroom accommodations and modifications. • Share questions, concerns, or feelings about intensive programming or services, such as occupational therapy.

GOAL SETTING

Purposeful goal setting is the key to efficient and productive conferences. Teachers who are reflective in their planning process are more likely to create goals that will lead to positive outcomes. Teachers should consider what will support the family's understanding of their child's strengths and needs and will foster collaborative action with families. Teachers should explore many factors as they set goals for the conference. The following are suggestions for how teachers can create thoughtful conference goals:

- **Link goals to the conference purpose.** Goals should always link back to the purpose for holding the conference. When the purpose is clear, setting the conference goals is straightforward.

- **State goals clearly.** Be sure that the goals can be explained in a way that makes sense to the family. Clear direction keeps the conference focused and organized.

- **Make practical goals.** The goals should have value for all conference attendees, including school and family members. Both entities should gain knowledge and understanding when the goals are achieved.

- **Limit conference goals.** Establishing too many goals for the conference can set all participants up for failure. Keep the conference goals to a reasonable number (two to four goals per conference meeting).

- **Create specialized goals for individual families.** While some goals are universal, each family deserves its own unique plan. Teachers should use their knowledge of family needs to develop practical, purposeful goals for every conference.

- **Solicit input from families.** Encourage families to share and reflect on their child's strengths, needs, and resources. Teachers can use family surveys, such as the Family Questionnaire (page 132), to suggest family-specific conference goals. Teachers may also incorporate conference discussion guides, such as the Family-Teacher Conference Documentation Gathering Tool (page 138), to set future conference goals with parents.

- **Consider flexibility.** Make goals adaptable to the conversation flow. Allow some flexibility in goal setting so that families will feel comfortable asking questions and sharing insights. To put this in perspective, think of the teacher who has set a conference goal of discussing scores on a communication screening. During the conference, the teacher outlines how the screening tool provides feedback on language development. As the teacher reviews data, the parent raises questions about how communication needs may affect her daughter's interaction with peers. A teacher who demonstrates flexibility will create a space to explore the parent's concerns both within and outside the scope of the screening results, rather than prioritizing her own interests above those of the family.

Supporting Family Needs

Parents balance many responsibilities in their daily lives. Obligations for work, family, and self can make it challenging for parents to fully commit to school partnerships. This is why recognizing family needs is a significant part of preparing for the school conference. When teachers can assist parents in temporarily isolating outside stressors, they create a dedicated space for productive useful dialogue. The result is more concentrated attention, participation, and engagement from families at school events. For conferences in particular, this level of focus is necessary for active listening and constructive problem solving.

When planning parent-teacher conferences, it's important to consider multiple family needs, with time being one of the most significant. Teachers should offer some flexibility in their conference scheduling. While most teachers are available directly after school hours, some parents may just be beginning their workday. Alternatively, children's extracurricular activities may make after-school hours inconvenient for meeting. To the best of their ability, teachers should offer a variety of conference meeting times before, during, and after the school day. In some cases, this means teachers may need to partner with colleagues, principals, or program directors to provide class coverage.

Similarly, some families may need conference setting options. While attending in person at the school may be an ideal space for sharing materials, documentation, and resources, other settings can be suitable for family meetings too. Some parents can be very intimidated by the school environment, and the classroom may trigger uncomfortable feelings. Other parents may not be able to attend in person because of transportation or work concerns. For these families, phone meetings or video conferencing may be more conducive to full engagement. Some pre-K programs may also support teachers who conduct conferences during home visits.

Families and teachers who do not speak the same language will require an interpreter to communicate effectively. When working with older students, teachers may be tempted to use the children themselves, or an older sibling, as the messenger. However, providing an interpreter is best practice because it offers the family the greatest opportunity for clear and respectful communication. Even when an interpreter is unavailable, teachers should always assume parents' competence. Limited understanding of the school language is never an indication of limited intelligence.

Beyond a language interpreter, some parents may need additional support persons. Other family members, caregivers, or resource personnel who spend time with the child may have unique perspectives that can further student progress in school. Additionally, some parents may want to bring friends or family as support for themselves. Keep in mind that difficult conferences can be just as worrisome for families as they are for teachers. A support person can be a source of comfort under tough circumstances. Teachers should be welcoming to all conference attendees and allow the parents to take the lead in encouraging their guests' participation.

When addressing family needs, flexibility is key. Make conscious efforts to acknowledge family pressures and to accommodate needs appropriately. At times, adjusting conference plans to honor family requests can be overwhelming or inconvenient. Nevertheless, the quality of the conference is always improved when both family members and teachers can bring their best selves to the conversation.

FAMILY INVOLVEMENT OR FAMILY ENGAGEMENT?

To achieve genuine collaboration, teachers must accept the family's role as partners in educating their children. Such a perspective begins with teachers embracing the tenets of family engagement in their conference planning. Educator Larry Ferlazzo (2011) describes *family involvement* as "leading with its mouth," identifying goals for the school, classroom, or child, and then informing families how they should contribute. On the other hand, Ferlazzo labels *family engagement* as "leading with its ears," as teachers prioritize listening to families.

Certainly, there is a place for both family involvement and family engagement in schools. Both approaches encourage families to be active in the learning community. However, in family-teacher conferencing, only engagement results in the family empowerment that fuels collaborative discussion and problem solving.

Planning for Collaboration

Partnership with families is necessary for student achievement in every area of growth. Many teachers enter conferences expecting to collaborate with parents but often fall short in their efforts. Collaboration is not promised simply because a family-teacher conference is scheduled. Like all other aspects of the conferencing process, teachers must prepare for successful collaboration.

Conferences are far less useful when teachers are the only attendees sharing information. Families, too, must be active participants in the communication process. Although some families will come to meetings with questions and insight prepared, others will be far less open about offering their ideas. Consequently, teachers need a repertoire of useful techniques to encourage participation in the conference discussion.

First and foremost, collaboration depends on both teachers and parents having opportunities to speak. This means that teachers must plan breaks in the conversation for families to process information, formulate questions, and build understanding. While the typical conference format is fast-paced and highly structured, planning short pauses in the conference provides a dedicated interval for families to offer their ideas. In preparing for the conference, it is important for teachers to reflect on where the discussion could benefit from a moment of quiet space.

Similarly, teachers may use a questioning protocol to motivate families to share their unique expertise. Such questions may explore family belief systems or highlight the child's strengths or interests. Integrating these questions in the conference design promotes family collaboration for multiple reasons:

- Tapping into the family's knowledge creates a sense of comfort and familiarity in the setting for both teachers and parents.
- Implementing questions builds parents' confidence in their capacity to contribute to their children's learning.
- The family perspective aids appropriate resource referrals and interventions for children.

See the following list for some questions that can promote collaborative engagement between teachers and families.

CONFERENCE QUESTIONS THAT BUILD COLLABORATION WITH FAMILIES

- Questions that promote comfort:
    - What do you and your child like to do for fun?
    - How are you and your child similar/dissimilar learners?
    - What does your child like about school?
- Questions that promote confidence:
    - What subjects do you enjoy learning with your child?
    - How do you help your child with homework?
    - What routine do you follow at mealtime/bedtime?
- Questions that promote resource sharing:
    - How can I support at school the behavior system you use for potty training at home?
    - What resources do you need to support your child's math skills?

Families who view themselves as integral to their children's progress are more likely to collaborate with teachers. When teachers take the time to acknowledge families' efforts in supporting their child's development and learning, family members are more eager to examine other ways to partner with the teacher. Planning a few positive comments about the family's engagement in school can go a long way toward building cooperative interaction.

Developing a Positive Teacher Mindset

One of the most effective strategies for preparing for a family-teacher conference is cultivating a positive mindset. At times, meetings with families can be unsettling, especially when the conversation focuses on student challenges. This is particularly true when the teacher is not quite sure how the family will respond to the shared information. In these cases, it is reasonable to be worried or nervous about meeting with family members. Nevertheless, maintaining a positive disposition sets an encouraging tone.

Regardless of the information shared, all conferences demand a great deal of focus and attention from teachers. This type of constant and persistent concentration is emotionally taxing. Before the conference begins, teachers should take some time for themselves. Taking short, strategic breaks during daylong conference scheduling provides a space for teachers to recharge between family meetings. Taking brief pauses to eat a meal, check messages, drink some water, or talk to a colleague is a good way to revive positive focus and energy for each meeting. As much as teachers may dislike sharing disappointing news with families, clear communication promotes informed decision-making. Sharing strengths *and* needs is a necessary part of supporting children's learning. Showing empathy is a useful way to keep the conversation positive and productive. Before each conference, reflect carefully on the information that will be shared. Consider the language that is used to describe the child and their work, and think about how this information would sound from the parents' point of view.

Griffin, a preschool child with autism, purposefully tears pages from classroom books. Griffin's teacher, Miss Ava, considers how she will discuss this concern with the family in an upcoming conference. Her first thought is to begin the conference with a list of incidents, peer and staff responses, and descriptions of damage. Miss Ava also thinks about continuing the conversation with a detailed explanation of how the behavior has negatively affected the child's social relationships followed by a stern ultimatum for the family to find a way to decrease the behavior or risk expulsion from the preschool center.

Before meeting with the family, Miss Ava reflects on the family's perspective. The family has reported book tearing at home, and Miss Ava knows that Griffin's parents are frustrated with the behavior as well. Hearing an itemized list of destroyed books or anecdotes of annoyed peers probably isn't going to help the family problem solve. Miss Ava ponders another approach. In the past, the family has always been willing to collaborate with teachers to shape Griffin's behavior positively. Miss Ava decides to start the conference by telling the family how much she appreciates this support and how she plans to continue to partner with them to navigate this concern as well.

As Griffin's family enters the conference, Miss Ava greets them with a pleasant demeanor. She talks about how much she enjoys Griffin's wonderful sense of humor and how happy it makes her and other staff to see his smiling face each morning. Next, Miss Ava acknowledges the stress that Griffin's behavior places on the family and thanks them for being willing to partner with her. Although Miss Ava doesn't

ignore the significance of the concern, she places far more emphasis on discussing practical solutions than rehashing past incidents. Consequently, the conference ends with a viable intervention plan for both home and school.

The conference with Griffin's parents was successful in part because Miss Ava placed herself in the shoes of the family. While she could not alleviate the family's stressors entirely, she could empathize with them, demonstrate positive regard for the child, and promote collaborative engagement. Collectively, these positive mindset behaviors stimulated productive outcomes with the family.

TIPS FOR A POSITIVE TEACHER MINDSET

- Visualize the conference going well. Instead of anticipating negative outcomes, think about all the ways the conference could end successfully.
- Reflect on positive student qualities. Ultimately, children should be at the center of conference discussions. Teachers should remind themselves, and the family, too, of the child's uniqueness through personal anecdotes about their learning.
- Teachers must consider the power of their words. When discussing the child's struggles, teachers should place themselves in the parents' position. Select words that demonstrate empathy and a commitment to progress.
- Engage in self-care. Teachers cannot care for others until they first show themselves sensitivity. Get plenty of rest and engage in healthy activities, such as exercise, heathy eating, and meditation. Use downtime in the conferencing schedule to replenish personal needs.
- Show self-compassion. Every teacher has missteps in the conference process; these errors are not a reflection of teaching competencies. Acknowledge mistakes, but do not allow them to overshadow the conference goals.

How to Use the Family-Teacher Conference Planning Tool

The Family-Teacher Conference Planning Tool is a place to design the major components of the conference. Writing ideas down in one collective space is a good way for teachers to organize their thoughts and to hold themselves accountable for the conference plan. However, be cautious; every conference should remain flexible and adaptable to attendees' needs. The planning form is not meant to serve as a checklist of conference activities but as a framework for the discussion.

Complete a separate conference planning sheet for each family. In this way, teachers have a personalized design for each meeting. Don't be discouraged if you do not have ideas for each planning area at the first attempt. Some aspects of the conference plan may require critical reflection. Begin with the conference purpose and goals and add the other components as you organize student data and/or family information.

Successful family-teacher conferences are built on careful and purposeful organization. Teachers who reflect on conference goals, family needs, and their own mindset before the first conference create comfortable spaces for dialogue and problem solving with parents to occur. Such open discussion promotes purposeful partnership between teachers and families, ultimately supporting student achievement. Chapter 3 will address how teachers can strengthen these professional relationships with families through a welcoming conference environment.

FAMILY-TEACHER CONFERENCE PLANNING TOOL

Student Name

Family Attending

Conference Date

Faculty/Staff Attending

Conference Purpose

Special Family Needs (check all that apply):

- ☐ Individualized Conference Scheduling
- ☐ Language Interpreter
- ☐ Additional Time
- ☐ Virtual/Phone Setting
- ☐ Supplemental Attendees
- ☐ Other ____________________

Conference Goals

Teacher-Directed Goals

Family-Directed Goals

Positive Student Notes

Academic

Behavioral

Social

Student Concerns

Concerns

Classroom Documentation

Family Questions

1. ____

2. ____

3. ____

CHAPTER 3

CREATING A WELCOMING CONFERENCE ENVIRONMENT

Parent-teacher conferences make me so nervous. I feel like I am always on guard for a sneak attack.

—PARENT OF A SECOND-GRADE STUDENT

Family-teacher conferences can conjure many feelings—excitement, happiness, anxiety, disappointment. School conferencing gives teachers the opportunity to share children's learning achievements and progress with the children's families. It is a time to celebrate the whole child, including success across academic, social, and behavioral domains. The school conference is also a place to discuss individual student needs, to give and receive feedback, and to develop plans for improvement.

Accordingly, feelings of apprehension and stress are common on both sides of the conference table. Even with thoughtful conference planning, moments of discomfort may be inevitable. For both families and teachers alike, some elements of the conference experience are difficult to anticipate. Critiques of their child can feel devastating for many families and may lead to a defensive response. Not knowing how families will respond to negative comments, some teachers may withhold important insight, stalling student advancement.

The feelings expressed in the parent quote at the beginning of this chapter should feel especially alarming to teachers. In this instance, the family member expresses a genuine insecurity in the conference setting. These feelings are certainly in contrast with positive family engagement. Just as students cannot do their best learning in an environment that feels unsafe, neither can families be open to genuine collaboration under distressing conditions. This is why developing a welcoming environment is crucial to successful family-teacher conferences.

Positive conferencing requires full engagement from both teachers and families. Teachers who ignore the importance of welcoming families into the classroom minimize the family's contribution to student success. Through a collection of small but intentional efforts, teachers can help families feel at ease. In doing so, teachers place the focus on professional relationship building and effective communication.

A welcoming environment is a gentle reminder that teachers and families are valuable members of a working partnership. Families who feel comfortable in the classroom are more likely to provide their insight and ideas to problem solve. Further, families who feel welcomed are more willing to assume positive intentions, rather than interpreting teacher behaviors as harmful or disinterested. Both these family attitudes lead to more productive and useful interaction during the conference setting, which supports student achievement inside and beyond the classroom.

Setting the Stage

Imagine it is your birthday and your friends and family have prepared a party for you. You wait in anticipation until the day of the celebration arrives. You enter the venue only to discover that the decorations reflect the taste of your friends. The party food is all your least favorite selections, and the music is loud and unpleasant by your standards. As you scan the room, the partygoers are unfamiliar and appear irritated or exhausted by your presence. Reluctantly, you take a seat as you anxiously await the presentation of birthday gifts. You are, however, disappointed again when you open a seemingly endless offering of trinkets that align more with the giver's style than your own. At the close of the party, you are left wondering what you may have done to your friends and family to prompt such an inhospitable response.

For some families, the described party experience mirrors the level of anxiety, confusion, and discomfort they feel before, during, and after a family-teacher conference. Although many families may approach the conference with hope and anticipation, from the first moments in the classroom, some parents encounter an environment that sends a very clear message that they are unwelcome and unvalued. Perhaps more significantly, families with these negative experiences begin to develop a narrative around schools and teachers that stifles the home-school partnership.

Far too often, teachers create conference settings that cater to their own comforts rather than those of the families. While teachers spend a great deal of time in their classrooms, the space is not theirs alone. The learning environment should be an inviting area for children and families alike. Within the conference setting, especially, teachers must consider the beliefs, backgrounds, and values of families. To avoid a situation similar to the depicted failed birthday party, teachers must be mindful of the comfort level of the "guests of honor."

Creating a welcoming environment for family-teacher conferences involves three critical aspects: physical, psychological, and social-emotional. The absence of even one of these elements can significantly affect the success of the conference. Welcoming classrooms promote productive collaboration, which is why teachers should consider how families may interpret and connect with the physical, psychological, and social-emotional environments.

THE PHYSICAL ENVIRONMENT

If you are asked to think of a classroom, the physical environment is probably the image that comes to mind first. The arrangement of furniture, classroom design, and available resources typically compose the physical environment. It seems logical that a pleasant and attractive physical space would support student engagement. A welcoming physical setting is equally important for family-teacher conferences.

When planning the meeting space, select furniture that is appropriate and flexible. While many early childhood teachers are content to sit in child-sized chairs or on a carpeted floor, most adults would find these seating options very uncomfortable–adult-sized chairs are a must! Whenever possible, use seating of equal heights to visually reinforce the idea that all conference participants have equivalent value and insight. Similarly, a rounded, rather than rectangular, table supports a collaborative atmosphere.

Another important element of the physical environment is the general classroom design. As a whole, the classroom should feel inviting to families. From a quick scan of the learning space, families should gather a general understanding of routines and values. Teachers should consider their teaching philosophy carefully and think about how the learning space can highlight their beliefs effectively. For instance, a well-stocked classroom library sends the message that literacy is a priority. Multiple displays of children's work suggest a student-centered teaching approach.

The classroom design should also highlight diverse perspectives and viewpoints. Posters, books, and displays reflecting different backgrounds and cultures can help families feel a sense of acceptance, value, and welcome that also communicates how teachers honor the cultures of individual students in the classroom.

PSYCHOLOGICAL AND SOCIAL-EMOTIONAL ENVIRONMENTS: WHAT'S THE CONNECTION?

The terms *psychological* and *social-emotional* are used in tandem so often that it can feel like the concepts are interchangeable. While the notions are connected in some ways, they encompass very different ideas with respect to the classroom environment.

In the conference setting, the purpose of the social-emotional environment is to create positive feelings for families through social interaction. The psychological environment, on the other hand, is a more holistic term vested in developing and sustaining confidence and trust in the conference process among families.

The report *Building Authentic School-Family Partnerships through the Lens of Social and Emotional Learning* (Skoog-Hoffman et al., 2023) suggests that teachers build trust with families through four basic actions:

- Listening
- Reflecting on power dynamics
- Reciprocal learning
- Collaborating to effect change

Engaging in these behaviors with families consistently affords teachers the best opportunity to build a positive psychological environment for families.

THE PSYCHOLOGICAL ENVIRONMENT

A positive psychological environment can go a long way toward establishing a sense of comfort among children's families. Trust is at the core of psychological security. Teachers, therefore, need to make efforts to connect with and develop working relationships with families before and after the conference. Establish routines that encourage open and honest communication not only at conference meetings but also throughout the school year. For instance, teachers may offer monthly drop-in hours for families to meet with the teacher to discuss concerns. They may also call one or two families each week to share positive messages about their children's progress. Printed materials, such as classroom newsletters or flyers, can also keep families informed of classroom activities, learning expectations, and family engagement opportunities. In these ways, teachers illustrate their investment in children's progress and achievements, increasing the likelihood that families will enter the conference with a positive, constructive mindset.

THE SOCIAL-EMOTIONAL ENVIRONMENT

A healthy psychological environment acknowledges families' social and emotional needs. At even the most basic level, collaboration requires a sense of connection among participants. This bonding is the goal of the social-emotional environment. While teachers should not attempt to build personal friendships with family members, they should convey a friendly disposition and a genuine interest in partnering with parents. Remember, respect is only earned when it is given. Teachers who want families to hear, process, and accept their insight must first show sensitivity to family social and emotional needs.

Aaliyah is a pre-K student who arrives late to school frequently. Her teacher, Miss Heather, wants to address this concern with Aaliyah's parents, but she knows a judgmental or critical approach will undermine a positive relationship with the family. Instead of accusing the family of ignoring the child's educational needs, Miss Heather states, "I've noticed that Aaliyah has been coming to school a little after the start of the school day. Is there anything I can do to support you during morning drop-off?" Such a teacher response demonstrates care and concern for not only the child but also for the family as a whole.

Families who encounter this level of care and concern in school interactions are more likely to share stressors and solicit support from teachers.

STRATEGIES TO CREATE WELCOMING PHYSICAL, PSYCHOLOGICAL, AND SOCIAL-EMOTIONAL ENVIRONMENTS

Strategies for a Positive Physical Environment

- Tidy the classroom. Organize materials and have student materials, resources, and/or documentation within easy access.
- Have multiple chairs available to accommodate unexpected family members or colleagues.
- Create a waiting space for early-arriving families. Offer light refreshments or reading materials for families to enjoy as they await their conference time.

Strategies for a Positive Psychological Environment

- Offer family engagement activities, such as volunteer activities, class visitations, and so on, before the school conference to build familiarity with you and the classroom.
- Demonstrate respect for families' schedules. Begin and end conferences on time.
- Establish regular opportunities through various means, such as phone, virtual, and in-person, to meet with families outside of school conferences.

Strategies for a Positive Social-Emotional Environment

- Involve families in relevant decision-making. Show respect for families' preferences even if they differ from your own choices.
- Express empathy for families. Show concern with verbal and nonverbal communication.
- Greet each family with genuine enthusiasm. Thank families for attending the conference.

Welcoming Culturally Diverse Families to Conferences

Culture is a broad concept that includes more than the race and ethnicity of children and their families. The National Association for the Education of Young Children (NAEYC) *Advancing Equity in Early Childhood Education* position statement defines culture as "the patterns of beliefs, practices, and traditions associated with a group of people" (2019). Some aspects of race may connect with the culture of your students' families. For example, some of Latinx families may identify as part of a Spanish-speaking culture. However, many aspects of culture are unrelated to ethnic heritage, such as the culture of single parents or families of children with specific health-care needs. Regardless of the cultural composition of their class, effective teachers engage in a wide variety of techniques to help families feel welcome in the school conference setting.

RECOGNIZING AND ADDRESSING BIASES

A bias is a strong opinion about a person, object, or behavior based on personal beliefs. Biases are natural among all people, families and teachers alike. Some biases are *explicit*. People are conscious of their explicit biases and make intentional choices based on these beliefs and feelings. For example, some people have an explicit bias toward dogs rather than cats. This bias would prompt these individuals to find dogs more loyal, safe, helpful, and cleaner than cats.

Other biases are *implicit*. This means individuals are unaware of the biases they hold but still make judgments based on their discriminatory beliefs. Teachers and families may have implicit biases about each other For instance, families may have biases about educators' teaching quality based on their age or years of experience. Similarly, teachers may undervalue a family's commitment to education based on a wide range of characteristics, including their household income, age, or education level.

Miss Kathie, a senior teacher at Little Hands Preschool, is an expert educator whom students and families adore. Yet she hasn't formed a connection with Nevaeh, the twentysomething parent of Jamarie, the newest child in her toddler classroom. At arrival and dismissal, Nevaeh keeps to herself. Miss Kathie often sees her rushing with Jamarie, watching videos on her phone with a single earbud cradled in her ear. Nevaeh rarely attends parent meetings and often comes to school in pajama pants and flip-flops. To Miss Kathie, Nevaeh seems distant and disinterested in her son's education. "Another irresponsible young parent," she thinks.

Several weeks later, Miss Kathie holds parent-teacher conferences in her classroom. Thinking Nevaeh will not attend her scheduled meeting, Miss Kathie is a little surprised when the parent arrives ten minutes early. Certain that Nevaeh will be inattentive, Miss Kathie plows through Jamarie's progress notes, making it difficult for Nevaeh to interject questions or comments.

As they wrap up, Nevaeh lingers at the conference table. "I know I always look like I am in a hurry in the mornings," she says almost apologetically. "I'm enrolled in a food service course at the community college, and I am training to be a manager at a local restaurant. Mornings are focused on getting Jamarie to school on time, and I try to spend as much time as I can with Jamarie in the afternoons before work in the evenings. But Jamarie really loves learning, and I want to do everything I can to keep him on track at school."

Miss Kathie feels a pang of guilt; she had convinced herself that because Nevaeh did not interact with her the way other families did, she was uninvested in Jamarie's education. Miss Kathie reflects on her biases and comes to the next conference meeting ready to partner with Nevaeh fully. Through this collaboration, Miss Kathie and Nevaeh find practical ways for Nevaeh and many other working families to participate in the learning community.

When biases are brought to the conference setting, they can interfere with open communication and stall problem solving. As seen in the preceding anecdote, biases can prompt teachers and families to devalue the other's interest and contributions to the discussion. Given the potential damage to positive relationship building, it is important that teachers reflect on their biases regularly. The following are some ideas for recognizing and addressing teacher biases:

- **Consider the source of biases.** Many biases are deeply rooted in early experiences and reinforced in daily activities. Reflect on your understanding of difference and its impact on your interaction with others.

- **Be humble.** In service roles such as teaching, errors in communication are inevitable. When biases emerge in conversations with families, be willing to hear families' interpretation of the exchange and apologize for causing hurtful feelings.

- **Demonstrate interest in learning.** While it can be tempting to rely on school families as a resource for studying cultures, it is not families' responsibility to build the teacher's cultural awareness. Instead, engage in self-directed research with high-quality publications, visual arts, and cultural venues. Teachers may explore local art museums, attend theater productions, visit houses of worship, engage with advocacy organizations, or participate in volunteer service events in the school community.

- **Explore new social groups.** Another way to grow knowledge is through interaction, conversation, and discussion with new communities. Explore groups that solicit participation from people of varied ages and backgrounds and who are vested in creating and sustaining equitable opportunities for children and youth.

- **Develop standardized decision-making practices.** Too often, teachers rely on feelings and "gut" responses to drive significant decision-making in the classroom. In these circumstances, bias takes the lead in making decisions about student evaluations and assessments, behavioral interventions, and discipline. Standardized checklists and rubrics set predetermined guidelines that promote fair and equitable decision-making.

ACKNOWLEDGING DIVERSE PERSPECTIVES

A classroom is filled with diverse ideas and perspectives. In the conference setting, it is the teacher's responsibility to create a safe space for all families to share their thoughts and ideas. Teachers' professional preparation can lead them to believe they are qualified to judge how some parents choose to raise their children. However, teachers are likely unaware of and have not experienced many aspects of a child's family life and background. This gap in understanding can make it challenging for teachers to fully comprehend how and why families make choices for their children.

Mrs. Harper has reached out to second-grade teacher Ms. Kline to discuss how her grandson, Liam, is progressing in math. At the conference, Ms. Kline shares that Liam seems to do well with one-on-one assistance but struggles when he has to work independently. She asks how Liam fares with completing math work at home. Mrs. Harper offers that Liam gets easily frustrated with homework, and both she and her husband frequently sit with him to assist with solving all the assigned problems.

Ms. Kline suggests that this approach may stall Liam's achievement in math. "He just needs to figure it out on his own," she says. "If you provide him too much help, he will never learn how to struggle with challenges."

Mrs. Harper frowns. "Maybe . . . but I'm afraid if we don't intervene at all, he will give up on learning math all together. His sister struggled with math in grade school and reinforced a lot of bad habits by not asking for help. Her confidence in math is completely broken now."

Ms. Kline responds, "Hmm. That's a good point. My students are learning many foundational skills in math this school year." On further reflection, Ms. Kline recalls that Liam has had more behavioral problems in math class lately. She wonders whether he may be overwhelmed with the classwork. "Perhaps we can try a compromise. Let's offer guided support for the first three problems to build Liam's confidence and security. Then, we can step away to leave him to do the rest on his own."

"That seems like a good idea," says Mrs. Harper, nodding, "but is it okay to intervene if Liam seems confused or upset about the work?"

"Of course," says Ms. Kline. "And don't forget to offer lots of praise and encouragement to Liam for working independently." Mrs. Harper nods in agreement. Ms. Kline schedules another conference meeting to revisit the plan in two weeks.

In this vignette, the educator viewed the conference from the family's perspective. To assume this role, teachers must be attentive listeners, reflecting on family messages and requesting clarification, as needed. This means that a family should have an opportunity to share their point of view and student-specific knowledge in every conference session. In this case, knowing the sibling's history with math outlined the motivation behind their concerns for Liam's school performance. Through hearing these types of family stories, teachers can gain a better understanding of the motivation for the family's decision-making for their child.

SUPPORTING LINGUISTICALLY DIVERSE FAMILIES

Growing diversity in contemporary communities has given rise to larger populations of students whose first language is something other than English. According to the National Center for Education Statistics (2024), 10.6 percent of students in U.S. public schools, or approximately 5.3 million children, were English learners in 2021. Although many schools have strong programming to support students learning English, teachers may be less knowledgeable of where to begin with engaging families who are linguistically diverse. In these cases, teachers may begin developing a repertoire of effective strategies from online teacher platforms, professional organizations such as NAEYC, or the National Clearinghouse for English Language Acquisition (NCELA). Often, linguistically diverse families are just as eager as native English speakers to support their children's learning. Teachers must create welcoming and inviting spaces where families who do not speak English fluently can participate fully in the school conference. Certainly, school interpreters are ideal for communicating across significant language barriers, but this resource may not always be available. In these circumstances, teachers may want to enlist a collection of other practices to help linguistically diverse families feel welcome.

TIPS FOR WELCOMING LINGUISTICALLY DIVERSE FAMILIES TO CONFERENCES

- Celebrate families' language diversity. Share with families the cognitive and social-emotional benefits of speaking multiple languages at a young age.
- Learn a few polite words and phrases, such as *thank you, welcome,* and *school,* to use in the conference session and/or to use in classroom displays. This is a very simple way to create a welcoming atmosphere.
- Limit the use of educational jargon and acronyms. These terms can often be difficult for any noneducator to grasp and may lead to confusion about the child's progress.
- Use student work and curricular materials to illustrate the child's present level of performance as well as grade-level expectations to the family.
- Make use of pauses throughout the conference discussion. Allow time for families to process information and ask questions.

SUPPORTING FAMILIES OF CHILDREN WITH DISABILITIES

Families who have children with disabilities may have some apprehension about participating in school conferencing. Worries about their child's academic, social, and behavioral progress sometimes accompany these families when they enter the conference setting. Similarly, some families may worry about how teachers and peers interact with their children. These fears can prompt uneasiness, placing families on the defensive long before the conference even begins.

Fortunately, there are effective methods for building rapport and welcoming families of children with disabilities to a conference. It can be especially powerful to begin the conference with appreciation for the families' support and partnership. Reassurance that the child is safe, happy, and productive in the classroom is a positive way to provide emotional security for the family as well. Additionally, as mentioned at the beginning of this chapter, the physical environment conveys significant messaging. No family wants to visit a classroom to find their child's desk separate from the other students'. Other evidence of inclusive practices, such as shared learning spaces and materials, can go a long way toward establishing a comfortable, welcoming conferencing environment for families of children with disabilities.

Welcoming Families in Virtual Conference Environments

Meeting individual needs is one of the most crucial ways teachers can welcome families. When families are feeling overwhelmed with child care, home responsibilities, and scheduling obligations, it is difficult for them to be fully present at a conference. Virtual conferences allow families to participate in a flexible format, as both the teacher and parent can opt to hold the conference in a comfortable and convenient time or space.

Yet merely holding the conference virtually is not enough to create a welcoming environment. In fact, teachers sometimes must work hard to make the virtual environment feel warm and inviting, rather than cold and clinical. As a result, the virtual conference setting has unique planning considerations, such as the following:

- **Logistical:**
  - Allow families an opportunity to self-select virtual conference times. Offer options outside of the typical business day to accommodate a wide variety of work schedules.

- Select a user-friendly but secure virtual platform that families can navigate easily. Offer printed directions to help troubleshoot common problems.

- **Technological:**
  - Activate safeguards, such as virtual waiting rooms or passcodes, that will keep families from entering another family's conference meeting.
  - Test the audio and video settings so families can see and hear the speaker.
  - Transfer student work and other data to a digital format so that information can be shared easily with families.

- **Personal:**
  - Check the room lighting to ensure that the family can connect visually with the teacher. Opt for a simple background that places the focus on the speaker.
  - Show genuine enthusiasm for meeting with the family. Greet the family as they enter the virtual environment. Thank the family for participating in the conference.
  - Be conscious of body language. Remember, virtual platforms focus on faces, so even minor facial expressions may appear magnified.

How to Use the Welcoming Classroom Checklist

Creating a welcoming environment for families requires intentional and thoughtful planning from the classroom teacher. While preparing for conference activity, it can be easy to lose track of the groundwork necessary to establish a setting of acceptance and warmth. The Welcoming Classroom Teacher Checklist is designed to remind teachers of significant criteria for a welcoming classroom.

The checklist organizes suggested responsibilities into three timeframes: one month before the conference, one week before the conference, and the day of the conference. Using these blocks of time as guidelines, teachers can revisit and reevaluate their efforts to welcome families to the conference setting. As every classroom has families of different backgrounds, this checklist will certainly fall short of outlining every aspect of a welcoming conference setting. Nonetheless, it is a starting place for teachers to reflect on their approach to building a comfortable environment for families to participate in productive conference engagement.

A welcoming environment is a strong motivation for functional family engagement. When families feel safe in the conference setting, they are more active participants. Welcoming families to the conference lets families know that teachers respect and value them as members of their children's support systems. This perspective promotes thoughtful dialogue and cooperative idea-sharing. Chapter 4 examines how active listening can enhance these two very essential elements of effective conferencing.

WELCOMING CLASSROOM TEACHER CHECKLIST

One Month Before the Conference

- □ Connect with each family via phone or in person at a school event.
- □ Provide opportunities for families to self-select conference meeting times.
- □ Explore technology platform options for virtual conferences.
- □ Learn the correct pronunciation of family names.
- □ Appraise the classroom decor, resources, and design for inclusive messaging and representation.

One Week Before the Conference

- □ Tidy the meeting environment.
- □ Secure appropriate seating options.
- □ Test virtual meeting platforms and equipment.
- □ Create a comfortable and engaging waiting space for families who arrive early.
- □ Forward personalized conference reminders (printed or digital) that underscore enthusiasm for meeting with families.

The Day of the Conference

- □ Demonstrate a friendly and welcoming disposition.
- □ Meet families at the classroom door.
- □ Greet each family by name.
- □ Escort families to the meeting space. Offer seating to all participants.
- □ Begin the conference with pleasantries that show care and concern for the family's well-being.

CHAPTER 4

ACTIVE LISTENING AND EFFECTIVE COMMUNICATION

She [the teacher] was so good at listening. It was like she heard things I couldn't make myself say.

—PARENT OF A CHILD WITH A DISABILITY

Listening and hearing are two very different skills. *Hearing* is the physical ability to take in sound from the world. *Listening*, on the other hand, describes the transformation of heard words into shared ideas. Although hearing is a biological practice, listening is a far more complicated endeavor. To listen effectively, the head and the heart must work together. As individuals listen, they build connections in their minds among personal thoughts, experiences, beliefs, and prior knowledge to create an understanding of what they hear. Yet, the process does not end there. An appropriate response is almost always dependent on emotional awareness and sensitivity.

Undoubtedly, effective teachers should be proficient at both receiving and understanding information. The classroom is a social space, and providing opportunities for students to share their thoughts and feelings is paramount to establishing a safe learning environment. Similarly, in the conference setting, teachers must create a space where families feel that their voices are heard and understood. This means that teachers cannot just hear the words that families share but also listen and respond in ways that show understanding. Such effective communication patterns build levels of comfort among families, prompting greater collaboration.

Developing productive communication habits can be challenging. Teachers are busy people, and listening requires quality time. As they focus on the goal of helping students and families, teachers with extensive classroom experience may fail to interpret each family story as unique. Instead, they may attempt to hurry ahead to a solution. However, listening well prioritizes understanding over responding. To truly connect with families, teachers must set aside their personal experiences and beliefs to embrace new perspectives and ideas. In this way, teachers can comprehend the strengths and needs of individual students and families.

The parent quoted at the beginning of this chapter reminds teachers that not all communication is verbal. In fact, families can say a lot without any words at all. Teachers who are focused and aware of family responses, both voiced and silent, can better understand the family's point of view. Through consistent positive interaction with families, teachers build a rapport that allows them to sense emotions, stressors, and concerns.

Additionally, getting to know children and their families develops a better understanding of learning goals. Open communication between teachers and families identifies the strengths and needs of the family. Through friendly interaction with families, teachers can uncover funds of knowledge (See chapter 1, p. 5) that they can integrate into action plans to support student success. Such a personalized approach to engagement creates a level of trust between families and teachers, which forms the basis for a foundation of participation and collaboration.

Active Listening

Traditional teaching requires a great deal of talking. Teachers are trained to provide information to different audiences through instruction, interaction, and collaboration. Each of these responsibilities involves speaking. Given these expectations, it is no wonder that talking competencies, rather than listening skills, play a central role in teacher preparation and evaluation. Listening, however, is absolutely essential to effective teaching. As such, teachers must learn and practice listening skills much the same as instructional strategies.

Effective listening is active listening. Active listening is more than listening to the words families share; it is also focusing on the emotions and behaviors families display. Teachers must give careful attention to body language and facial expressions to understand the family perspective fully. The teacher's focus must be free from outside distractions and responsibilities. Similarly, active listening is nonjudgmental. The initial goal of every conference is not to problem solve concerns but to provide a space for families to feel seen. When teachers use it properly, active listening sends a message that families are valued not just for what they say and do but also for who they are.

Mr. Leon is an experienced pre-K teacher. Ms. Watson, the parent of one of the children in the classroom, has scheduled a conference to discuss a kindergarten transition plan for her daughter Kristie. Mr. Leon has prepared for the conference by gathering an abundance of portfolio data, including assessment scores, student work, and classroom photos.

As Mr. Leon greets Ms. Watson at the classroom door, he immediately notices that her demeanor is distinctly different from previous encounters. Her shoulders are hunched, and her gaze drifts downward. At the beginning of the conference, she barely acknowledges photos of Kristie from the pumpkin patch field trip that Mr. Leon shares with her. Yet, as an active listener, Mr. Leon is attuned to both parents' words and behaviors. He recognizes that Ms. Watson is distracted from the conference. In response, he moves the piles of student documentation to the side of the table, leans forward, and places his hands quietly in his lap. Then he says, "I appreciate you coming in for our conference. I want to make this time most useful for you. Are there concerns about Kristie that you would like to discuss now?"

His gentle, open body language and compassionate voice create a sense of comfort for Ms. Watson. She sighs softly and starts to share some of the problems her older child experienced when he entered kindergarten. Ms. Watson is concerned that Kristie will struggle with the adjustment as well. Mr. Leon listens silently, nodding and maintaining eye contact as she speaks. He avoids interrupting or responding until Ms. Watson completes her thoughts.

Mr. Leon highlights Kristie's academic strengths and needs. The teacher and the parent discuss strategies to support Kristie in the kindergarten classroom, such as connecting with the new teacher the first weeks of school and taking Kristie to visit the school building in August. Ms. Watson still feels nervous about the changes ahead, but she is hopeful about the plan that she and Mr. Leon have prepared for the transition.

By reading Ms. Watson's body language and responding with nonverbal cues, Mr. Leon showed he valued the parent as a person and respected her concerns. Although he had a planned conference agenda, he prioritized the family's needs and, in doing so, created a comfortable and secure space for collaboration. Through this type of family-teacher interaction, positive partnerships are developed and sustained.

BENEFITS OF ACTIVE LISTENING IN THE CONFERENCE SETTING

During a conference, active listening to families leads to productive outcomes. Families who have teachers who listen to them are more likely to continue talking, leading to a depth and richness in child-specific knowledge. Parents are the keepers of valuable information about their children's learning strengths, preferences, and interests. When they feel they can freely share this information with their children's teachers in the conference setting, families are better able to partner with teachers to support student progress. Teachers can then use this knowledge to design individual student instructional goals.

LISTENING LEADERSHIP

In a 2020 article, educational leader Nicole Furlong discusses an inquiry-based form of active listening that she names "Listening Leadership." The goal of Listening Leadership within the teacher-family relationship is to create consistent opportunities to listen to families' stories to promote information gathering. This insight is helpful as families and teachers work together to explore potential procedures and systems to address underserved needs.

Consider how the Listening Leadership approach might be applied to study low attendance rates for family-teacher conferences. Instead of assuming disinterest, teachers could connect with families directly through multiple means, such as text, email, home visits, personal conversations, surveys, and so on, to learn what barriers exist for families. Reflecting on these "data," teachers could investigate more equitable conferencing methods. By including families in the developing and implementing of programming, Listening Leadership prioritizes family belonging in schools.

Families who feel heard during their interactions with teachers develop their agency as decision-makers for and with their children. Teachers who listen validate families' feelings, thoughts, and ideas. Such affirmation helps families to recognize their contributions to the conferences as relevant and valuable. As teachers engage in active listening, families are empowered to offer suggestions and recommendations to enhance progress and navigate problems. Families may be more willing to share feedback on teacher input as well, creating more effective support for students. In this way, active listening prompts dynamic participation from all conference stakeholders.

OVERCOMING LISTENING ROADBLOCKS IN THE CONFERENCE SETTING

Teachers—and families—may face some challenges when using active listening. Even when both sides are attentive listeners, stakeholders can misunderstand or misinterpret each other's messages. Teachers can misread cues from family members; parents can misconstrue a teacher's tone or phrasing. A disconnect in understanding can easily lead to a breakdown in communication. When teachers sense confusion or frustration in a discussion, it is best to take a pause from the conference to ask clarifying questions or provide additional context.

Educational jargon, too, can fuel miscommunication and misunderstandings between teachers and families.

Ms. Young, preschool teacher, mentions to a parent that his daughter is benefiting from differentiation instruction. In explaining her approach, she shares how the child works in a small group weekly to practice letter writing with a sensory tray of sand and shaving cream as other children practice writing letters on paper. The parent, unfamiliar with the term "differentiated instruction," becomes agitated, thinking his daughter is being labeled for special education services without his consent. This miscommunication develops misdirected fears, creating lingering feelings of mistrust between the parent and teacher.

Self-regulation can be another challenge of active listening. Some very delicate issues can be at the center of school conference discussions. While families are generally protective of their children, teachers can be similarly sensitive to critiques of their professional efforts. When either group feels confronted, their feelings of frustration can translate to harsh or undesirable responses. Teachers must remain in control of their emotions.

Lastly, teachers need to be mindful that active listening is not always solution driven. As members of a service profession, many teachers have a strong desire to be helpful. However, active listening is not about solving families' problems. Instead, it is about offering an opportunity for families to share concerns, beliefs, and feelings openly without criticism. Active listening should also lead to strong teacher-family partnerships where both stakeholders feel empowered to offer insight and to contribute to decision-making.

Strategies for Active Listening

To connect well with families, teachers may need to employ several active listening strategies simultaneously. Effective active listening depends on understanding and processing different types of information and requires close monitoring of situational and personal awareness. The following active listening strategies can prove useful in the conference setting:

- **Be present.** Conference meeting days are extremely busy for teachers. The stressors of maintaining a schedule, preparing documentation, and meeting families for the first time can feel overwhelming. Staying focused on families' insight is crucial for active listening. Teachers should take note of their attention levels during interaction with families, redirecting themselves as necessary.
- **Monitor nonverbal cues.** Body language can be highly expressive. Teachers should listen not only to what family members share with words but also what they suggest through posture, voice inflection, and facial expressions.
- **Request clarification.** If a parent shares something that feels unclear, ask for additional context or information. In natural breaks in the conversation, take time to confirm information. Restate or paraphrase key aspects of the conversation and ask families to verify underlying ideas.
- **Postpone judgment.** The goal of active listening is to understand. As families are speaking, focus on their words rather than a response. Be open to thoughts and ideas, and hold back on criticism. Allow families to share without interruptions or arguments.
- **Be self-aware.** During the conference, teachers should be aware of what their body language or facial expressions may be conveying. Defensive body

positioning and behaviors, such as crossed arms, eye rolling, leaning back, and so on, often communicate disinterest. Open body positioning and behaviors, such as leaning in, head nodding, and direct eye contact, are more likely to signal engagement.

Integrating these strategies supports collaborative conferencing efforts. The following two scenarios describe how a preschool and first-grade teacher may respond using some of the active listening techniques described in the preceding section.

A grandparent shares concerns about her pre-K grandchild interacting with peers who play too roughly with him.

Teacher's Response Using Active Listening:

- **Be aware:** "It sounds like your grandchild feels unsafe in school because some of his friends play too physically with him during group times."
- **Request Clarification:** "Can you tell me more about the rough behavior that your grandson experiences when he is playing with his friends? Has this been an ongoing concern, or is this a recent issue?"
- **Acknowledge Nonverbal Cues and Feelings:** "I understand how upsetting it can be when you are worried about your child's well-being at school. It's natural to want them to feel safe."
- **Postpone Judgment:** "I have noticed that some of our students engage in rough-and-tumble activity in their imaginative play. I certainly can monitor these interactions more closely. We may also work together to encourage your grandson to communicate to his friends when their behaviors make him feel uncomfortable."

A parent of a second-grade student discusses his son's failing spelling grades and the child's frustration with completing writing assignments at home.

Teacher's Response Using Active Listening:

- **Being Present:** "Thank you for being willing to meet with me about this concern. I am glad that we were able to schedule a time when we both can focus on how to help your child. I would like to take notes during our meeting so that we will have a record of our plans to support your son."
- **Request Clarification:** "It sounds like you're really worried about your son's spelling grades and the stress that writing independently seems to be causing your child. Is that correct?"
  "Can you tell me more about what your child says about his writing assignments at home?"
- **Acknowledge Nonverbal Cues and Feelings:** "I can see how that situation is worrisome for both you and your child. I recognize how difficult it must be to see your child struggle with his schoolwork."
- **Postpone Judgment:** "It is very clear that education is important to your family, and you want your child to do well in school. It sounds like you're trying very hard to support your child at home. I want to partner with you. I would like to work one-on-one with your son to provide extra practice with spelling words. I can also adjust his writing homework to provide him with some writing success and to build his confidence."

By actively listening, the teachers not only validate the family concerns but also create a partnership aimed at addressing student needs. This approach helps families to feel seen and heard in the conference setting. In this way, families are empowered to contribute readily to problem-solving efforts.

Effective Communication

Although active listening is important, almost no family members expect to attend a conference where they do all the talking. Family-teacher conferences should follow a give-and-take model, where both parties contribute to the conversation. Families expect teachers to provide information specific to their child's progress; to do so effectively, teachers must have strong communication skills. When information is disorganized or unclear, it is difficult for others to process and understand. Incoherent messages serve little to no purpose in decision-making and often leave families feeling confused and frustrated.

Teachers who have strong communication skills are better poised to inform families of critical information. They provide insight into student strengths and needs in a way that is both direct and accessible. Teachers are responsible for sharing not only important information but also the value of that information in the context of children's school success. Teachers use good communication skills to facilitate productive discussions and shared perspectives.

ONE- AND TWO-WAY COMMUNICATION

Communication within the classroom comes in two forms: one-way and two-way. As the name suggests, one-way communication offers information from one direction and emphasizes reporting rather than discussion. Two-way communication, on the other hand, is conversation based, with a focus on dialogue. All stakeholders have an opportunity to provide insight and feedback.

One-way communication can serve a purpose in the conference setting. At times, the teacher will need to take the lead in reviewing documentation, data, or policies. In some cases, one-way communication may take the form of documentation sent home to families ahead of the conference. If families have limited familiarity with these materials, they may need to rely on the teacher's verbal or written guidance to build understanding. One-way communication gives parents a chance to develop their awareness of student performance indicators and learning expectations.

The *Principles of Effective Family Engagement* by NAEYC (n.d.) recommend two-way communication for school-home interaction, including family-teacher conferences. This approach allows for questioning, clarification, and collaborative problem solving. Additionally, two-way communication helps teachers and families explore different perspectives and ideas, making it easier to navigate disagreements. The following list offers teachers examples of how to integrate these types of communication in conferencing planning, implementation, and follow-up.

Before the conference:

- One-way communication:
  - Classroom newsletters providing details about conference procedures
  - Automatic phone announcements reminding families of conference dates/hours
  - Teacher directories with listings of qualifications, experience, and expertise
  - Instructions for scheduling conferences
  - School websites with curriculum information, benchmark testing procedures, grading policies
- Two-way communication:
  - Home visits to determine goal setting
  - Home-school notebooks for providing daily reports on student progress
  - Interactive school apps for sharing photos of learning activities
  - Family phone calls to remind families about conference appointment times and to encourage participation

During the conference:

- One-way communication:
  - Explanation of testing protocols and measures
  - Review of school procedures for routine issues, such as tardiness, behavioral consequences, early dismissals, program hours, and so on
  - Description of classroom or learning center organization
  - Clarification of the structure and design of report cards or progress reports
- Two-way communication:
  - Discussion of appropriate student goals
  - Collaborative problem solving with respect to student concerns
  - Highlighting student strengths and needs in the learning environment

After the conference:

- One-way communication:
  - Delivery of conference notes kept during the meeting for record keeping
  - Release of school or classroom handbook
  - Flyers for upcoming school events or volunteer opportunities
  - Documentation of signed paperwork or school forms
- Two-way communication:
  - Virtual meetings to revisit and revise student goals
  - Updates on instructional strategies or behavioral interventions
  - Family workshops to address common training needs among families

COMMUNICATION STYLES

Communicating with families is a complicated endeavor. In school conference settings, teachers sometimes must be the bearers of difficult news. Sharing information about student challenges can place teachers in uncomfortable situations where family responses are not always receptive or predictable. Feelings of vulnerability and shame can prompt families to direct frustrated feelings at teachers. However, teachers still have an obligation to be forthcoming with accurate information about their students. Adopting an appropriate communication style can support constructive conferencing.

There are multiple ways to communicate with families at conferences. Some educators assume a passive approach. Passive communication positions the families' feelings above message sharing. Such a response minimizes the attention and support that the family can direct to addressing the student challenge. Further, passive communication is particularly frustrating for families when seemingly "minor" behaviors escalate quickly.

At the opposite end of the spectrum is aggressive communication, which prioritizes message sharing above appropriate regard for the families' feelings. An aggressive communication approach fails to demonstrate care or concern. This communication style often blames families solely for the student concern, failing to recognize the teacher's role in supporting the student and family. Teachers who consistently engage in aggressive communication place their positive relationships with families at risk.

A third approach, an assertive communication style, values both honesty and sensitivity. Assertive communication is an ideal communication style for conferences because it balances professional responsibilities and personal connections appropriately. Teachers who communicate assertively stress the seriousness of the concern but are aware of the family's response and demonstrate appropriate sensitivity. Consider the differences among passive, aggressive, and assertive communication styles in the following vignettes.

A teacher and parent are meeting about Jasmine, a child who frequently takes toys away from peers during playtime. Mr. Ross, a teacher with a passive communication style, fears upsetting the family. Consequently, Mr. Ross only casually mentions the incidents, providing limited details about the behavior. Further, Mr. Ross rushes to the next topic of discussion, providing no time for the parent to respond to the concern, suggest reasons for the behaviors, or discuss possible solutions. Believing the incident is an isolated occurrence, the family sees no need to partner with Mr. Ross to support Jasmine. The next day in the classroom, the behavior continues, but Jasmine has now begun pushing peers to take their toys.

Ms. Lisa, a teacher with an aggressive communication style, also holds a conference with Jasmine's family. In discussing Jasmine's difficulty sharing, Ms. Lisa bluntly tells the family that Jasmine's behavior is unacceptable. Ms. Lisa begins the conference with a list of incidents, peer and staff responses, and descriptions of damaged toys. Despite noticing that the parent is visibly upset, Ms. Lisa continues the conversation by describing worst-case-scenario effects of the behavior on the child's social relationships and academic learning. The teacher also sets an ultimatum for the family to decrease the behavior or risk expulsion from the program. Feeling blamed and judged for her child's behavior, the parent immediately becomes defensive, criticizing the teacher's interventions and interaction with her child. When Ms. Lisa schedules another conference for the following month, the parent does not attend.

Ms. Ruthie, a teacher with an assertive communication style, leads a third conference with the family. She discusses Jasmine's behavior concerns openly and honestly. Ms. Ruthie begins the conversation with positive notes about the child and gratitude for the family's investment in Jasmine's education. Following, Ms. Ruthie shares the behavioral concern with the parent directly, offering contextual insight and specific examples of Jasmine's challenges with sharing. When Ms. Ruthie begins to see the parent appear confused and worried, she pauses to address questions and discuss concerns. As the parent grows anxious and upset, Ms. Ruthie reassures the family that she will support Jasmine in the classroom. During the conference meeting, Ms. Ruthie and the family work collaboratively to develop a plan for directly teaching

prosocial skills along with appropriate rewards and consequences for Jasmine. At the close of the month, Jasmine has made significant improvements in her sharing skills.

Mr. Ross's passive communication style led to miscommunication, hindering collaborative guidance and support for Jasmine. Without these resources, Jasmine's behaviors quickly became more destructive. Passive communication also often leads to a lack of trust and transparency, with families feeling that the teacher has misinformed them purposefully. If Mr. Ross continues with this communication approach, he can expect his relationship with the family to diminish.

Ms. Lisa's aggressive communication style had a more immediate negative effect on the school-home partnership. Her focus on Jasmine's negative behaviors, lack of empathy for the family in the presence of clear indicators of distress, and expulsion threats created an environment of confrontation. Showing limited empathy during the meeting, Ms. Lisa placed blame with the family, ignoring her role in supporting the child. No longer feeling like a member of a partnership, the parent became disengaged and disinterested in collaboration.

In stark contrast to both the passive and aggressive styles, Ms. Ruthie's assertive communication was respectful to the family. She captured a full picture of the child by beginning the conversation with positive insight. Her explanation of the concern was clear and direct. Further, Ms. Ruthie was skilled at reading the emotions of the family and responded appropriately with empathy and support. In this way, the parent felt heard and understood, empowering her to work with the teacher to problem solve.

As illustrated in these vignettes, how a teacher chooses to communicate can affect student success and family relationships. However, teachers should note that only the assertive communication style led to positive outcomes for the students. Using assertive communication, the teacher used direct language to address the concerns, monitor family input, and provide constructive feedback in a way that promoted understanding and collaboration

TIPS FOR ASSERTIVE COMMUNICATION IN CONFERENCE SETTINGS

- Speak factually about the concern. Offer documentation with specific details about the situation, including dates, times, antecedents, and consequences. Provide data about the behavior patterns or frequency.
- Focus on the individual child. Share how the behaviors affect the child's progress in the classroom. Limit discussion about how the behavior affects other children or adults in the classroom.
- Avoid blaming the family for student concerns. Assist families with viewing the behavior through a developmental lens.
- Reassure families of your commitment to the child's progress. Collaborate with the family to identify strategies to stimulate progress.
- Monitor families' responses for signs of significant distress. If families appear to be visually upset, offer a break or an alternative time to continue the conversation.
- Acknowledge the present level of interest or support for the concern. Remember, simply taking the time to meet to discuss progress is a significant effort for some families.

UNDERSTANDING HIGH-RISK RESPONSES

A "high-risk" response can hinder effective conversation by cultivating negative feelings. In their text *Reflective Listening*, authors Neil Katz and Kevin McNulty (1994) identify three different types of high-risk responses: evaluating, solving, and withdrawal.

- **Evaluating:** This approach centers the family's message around the teacher's own value system of right and wrong, good and bad, pleasing and disappointing. Evaluating diminishes the family's capacity to assess and understand their own thoughts and feelings. By limiting open communication, an evaluating high-risk response can significantly damage a family's sense of belonging in the conference setting. Consider the following examples:
  - "That's a poor parenting choice." This response places blame on the family member.
  - "Your response is unreasonable." What may seem unreasonable to the teacher may feel appropriate to the family.
  - "You're being too sensitive." It may be difficult for families to separate their feelings for their child from their feelings about the concern.
- **Solving:** The teacher assumes control for problem solving the family's concern. This approach deprives the family of the sense of agency in making their own choices and prevents them from having genuine accountability in decision-making. Both these consequences have long-term effects, as families who learn to rely on teachers for problem solving are unlikely to be active participants in future school conferencing. Consider the following examples:
  - "I strongly recommend . . ." Teacher recommendations do not give families an opportunity to contribute to problem solving.
  - "Your only option is . . ." As this response plainly suggests, families cannot explore other choices.
  - "That's your job as a parent." Family-teacher relationships should be a partnership. Problem solving should be collaborative.
- **Withdrawal:** This high-risk response attempts to protect the teacher from upset feelings. A withdrawal response strives to place the teacher at ease by dismissing the central issue as insignificant, fleeting, or fixable. Teachers who use withdrawal high-risk responses in conferences cannot demonstrate empathy with families. A lack of compassion distances teachers not only from parents' concerns but also from the families themselves. When teachers do

not make efforts to connect with families, communication systems break down quickly. Consider the following examples:

- "Everything will be fine." Some concerns do not resolve themselves as expected. Families may need to prepare themselves for significant changes.
- "You don't need to worry about that." Seemingly minor events to teachers can be worrisome to families. Teachers should recognize all feelings.
- "Things could be much worse." While some situations could indeed be worse for families, teachers should never classify distress.

Although high-risk responses may make families feel better temporarily, they rarely empower or support families. Whether intentional or not, high-risk responses can be offensive and stifle productive conversation too. Further, the use of high-risk responses shifts attention from the needs and wants of the family to those of the teacher. Alternatively, teachers should make efforts to reflect families' feelings through clarifying statements and/or follow-up questioning. In contrast to high-risk responses, both these options demonstrate care and concern for the family. Consider the following:

- Instead of "That's a poor parenting choice," try "I know you're doing your best for your child."
- Instead of "Your response is unreasonable," try "Tell me more about . . ."
- Instead of "You're being too sensitive," try "I appreciate your feedback about ________________. Can you give me an example of ______?"
- Instead of "I strongly recommend ________________," try "How would you like to move forward? One thought I have is . . ."
- Instead of "Your only option is ________________," try "Let's consider our choices."
- Instead of "That's your job as a parent," try "Would you like to brainstorm ways we can work together to figure this out?"
- Instead of "Everything will be fine," try "How can I support your child/family?"
- Instead of "You don't need to worry about that," try "What is worrying you about . . ."
- Instead of "Things could be much worse," try "It seems that you are feeling ________________."

Soliciting Family Insight

Even when teachers demonstrate strong listening and communication skills, families may be reluctant to express their point of view. Some families still consider school conferences as solely a teacher-directed meeting. Yet the depth of collaboration is so much richer when families coordinate expertise and knowledge. Certainly, no teacher can force a parent to provide insight during a conference, but teachers can use strategies to encourage active engagement from families.

- **Pause.** Family-teacher conferences cover a large amount of content. Many families will need time to process information and build understanding. Teachers should integrate brief pauses in conferencing to solicit feedback or questions from families. While a break in conversation may feel awkward at first, it may be necessary to give families time to collect their thoughts.
- **Ask open-ended questions.** Questions with yes-or-no answers will rarely prompt others to elaborate on their feelings or ideas. By contrast, probing questions can encourage family members to open up about their experiences. Further, teachers can motivate families to extend their responses to these questions by incorporating follow-up questions, requesting examples, or offering nonverbal reassurance, such as by nodding or smiling.
- **Solicit family-specific information.** Within the conference setting, there is some family-specific insight that can be particularly useful to the teacher. For instance, the conference may be a good time to discuss the family's strengths, traditions, or general goals for their child. As these topics are areas of expertise for the family, they may be comfortable sharing this information with teachers. See "Conference Questions That Build Collaboration with Families" on page 25 for suggested family-specific questions.
- **Acknowledge support.** Compliments can be a kind way to recognize families' efforts and solicit additional information. Many student successes in the classroom are the results of effective family-teacher partnerships. Beginning the conference with gratitude for the family's role in the child's progress may stimulate discussion about learning supports in the home setting.
- **Provide data.** Data can be a very powerful conversation starter. Portfolios, for instance, that illustrate student progress over time can be exciting for families to review. Teachers can ask families to share their thoughts on student growth and their goals for ongoing progress.

Using the Effective Conference Communication Practicing Tool

The following conference vignettes are designed to provide teachers with practice constructing high-quality responses that demonstrate professional competence, social awareness, and sensitivity. After reading each vignette, teachers should reflect on their replies, noting pitfalls, such as high-risk responses, along with opportunities to support families through care and empathy. Teachers may consider partnering with a colleague, with each educator taking on either the teacher or parent role in each scenario. Through role-play, teachers can use this tool to practice active listening and perspective sharing.

Strong communication skills are key to productive conferencing. Teachers should make every effort to help families feel heard and understood in their school interactions. In this way, families develop a secure connection with teachers, increasing active participation and engagement in conferences. Chapter 5 will offer ways to pair this effective communication with appropriate document sharing to promote productive conferencing.

EFFECTIVE CONFERENCE COMMUNICATION PRACTICING TOOL

1. Using an Assertive Communication Style

For many families, teachers serve as a resource for understanding developmentally appropriate and grade-level expectations. Teacher expertise in child development and instructional practice, coupled with child-specific knowledge, helps families make informed decisions. Also, an assertive communication style supports families' confidence in teacher knowledge and skills. How could a teacher employ an assertive teaching style in this situation?

> Kristina has been struggling in your first-grade class. With intensive, one-on-one teaching, Kristina can now recognize all letters and most letter sounds. Despite this progress, you are still concerned that Kristina will not meet grade-level standards by the close of the school year, and you believe retention is necessary.

Notes:

2. Asking Open-Ended Questions

Open-ended questions encourage families to elaborate on their ideas and thoughts. Pointed questions can clarify understanding and illuminate the underlying issue. How might open-ended questions highlight the driving force behind this parent's concern?

> Jakob is a student in your pre-K classroom. Recently, Jakob's father has scheduled a conference with you. When he arrives, he is visibly upset. "Jakob comes home crying every day," he begins the conversation. "Why don't you like my son?"

Notes:

3. Confirming Understanding

Asking questions, paraphrasing ideas, and summarizing central themes are all useful ways teachers can confirm family messaging in the conference setting. Taking time to verify what is said maintains the integrity of the conference. In what ways might a teacher confirm understanding in these circumstances?

> Rashawn is a new student in your second-grade classroom. His mother is concerned about his transition to the new district. During the conference, she mentions that he does not talk about friends, complains of being "bored" at recess, and now is reluctant to go to school.

Notes:

CHAPTER 5

COLLECTING APPROPRIATE DOCUMENTATION

I have no idea what it means when you say my child has "off-task behaviors," and if I don't know what you're saying, I can't help.

—PARENT OF A PRE-K STUDENT

One key benefit of family-teacher conferences is the chance to collaborate side by side with families. These meetings let families and teachers explore ways to support student learning and development. To have this type of positive influence on student success, both teachers and families need a clear understanding of children's current strengths and needs. That's why information sharing is so crucial at these conferences.

Discussion alone is not enough to build a deep and rich understanding of student progress. Given their unique backgrounds and expertise, teachers and families sometimes hold different assessments of student learning. Further, the parent quote at the beginning of this chapter points out that the language teachers use to express concerns about students can sometimes be unclear to families. The terms that teachers use in their description of student behaviors can have multiple meanings that cannot be defined with words only. As expressed in the quote, such confusion can leave families feeling helpless to contribute to their children's skill advancement.

Fortunately, documentation of student progress adds transparency to the conference process. By incorporating documentation as a resource in conferences, teachers provide practical evidence of student learning. Documentation translates school standards and teacher expectations into concrete skill sets and provides families with visual interpretations of complex developmental milestones. For instance, concepts such as fine motor development become clearer with student work samples to illustrate skills. With such detailed understanding, families can identify techniques for addressing their children's concerns. Having a role in instructional planning gives families genuine agency in educational decision-making.

Documenting a child's growth cannot be a haphazard practice, and teachers must be intentional in their data-collection procedures. Documentation that teachers collect over time and across settings is reliable and useful. From these records, teachers and families can discover important patterns that help them make informed decisions. In cases where a teacher must share concerns about a child, the family can sometimes have a hard time accepting that their child may be struggling and need support. Documentation offers important data and places the focus on problem solving with the family rather than on convincing them that a struggle exists.

Sharing documentation should be as much a part of conferences as interacting with families. Teachers who are well prepared for conferencing use a "show and tell" approach to describe student progress. Without either of these elements—showing and telling—teachers are at a distinct disadvantage as they explain student strengths and needs. Gaps in understanding can prevent families from providing valuable insights about their child.

Student Documentation

Student documentation is a record of student strengths and needs. Although simple in description, gathering data requires a purposeful approach. Studying a child's learning patterns involves considering a variety of factors that can influence student achievement. Teachers should examine both the processes and products of student learning as well as the circumstances that shape child behaviors. Teacher actions, too, can affect student responses. When teachers assemble work samples with this level of direction, documentation can systematically address specific inquiries about student learning.

Documentation has many roles in conferencing. Most often, teachers may consider documentation as evidence of student achievements and challenges. It should tell a story of student growth over time and in various settings. For teachers and families alike, documentation should prompt reflective thinking and planning. Perhaps most importantly, student documentation should inform instructional practices and affirm educational decision-making. In this way, student documentation becomes a "call to action" rather than simply a listing of behaviors.

BENEFITS OF STUDENT DOCUMENTATION

Certainly, student documentation is valuable in the family-teacher conference, but there are also important benefits for all stakeholders outside of school meetings. As teachers collect student data, they become more knowledgeable of each student as an individual. Such information helps them better understand and meet a child's needs. Reviewing documentation before the conference helps teachers be better prepared to discuss student growth within the classroom. Insight from student documentation can help teachers set the goals for conferencing, making efficient use of the meeting time.

From the family's perspective, student documentation creates a visual illustration of learning. This representation is especially important for showcasing the development of the whole child. With a wide collection of student documentation, families can see growth in their child's cognitive, social, physical, and behavioral learning. Additionally, even with a single sample of student work, families can make interpretations of student persistence, curiosity, and maturity alongside academic performance.

The visual evidence of student learning can also help families gain a deeper understanding of student work. Goals for young children in today's classrooms are quite different from the goals teachers had for their parents' generation. As a result, families may not be aware of the developmental milestones for early childhood. By providing guidance, teachers can offer families a clearer picture of their children's learning outcomes. This insight helps families support their children more effectively.

Seeing their growth over time is valuable for students too. When teachers and families include the children in the discussion of their work, they convey respect. Students are more likely to take their learning seriously when teachers and families explain the relationship between their efforts and progress in the classroom. These conversations encourage students to assume greater ownership in their learning. Students who see themselves as capable and competent learners are more committed to learning.

Types of Documentation

Student documentation can take different forms. Some conferences may incorporate universal documentation for all students. For example, many families of elementary children would expect to review a report card at a conference held at the close of a grading period. Families of preschool children, on the other hand, may assume that teachers would share a developmental checklist at a biyearly conference. However, the types of documentation teachers use in conferencing can be more student specific. The goal of the conference should determine what documentation the teacher shares with the family. Teachers may incorporate the following documentation forms in conferencing activities:

- **Student work:** This is a collection of examples of daily activities from the classroom. These materials provide families with guidelines of some age- or grade-level expectations.
- **Photographs:** Photographs of students engaged in school routines or learning tasks offer families a glimpse of daily class procedures. Photographs may also showcase student project work.
- **Assessments:** Tests are a familiar form of documentation to families. Assessments provide practical feedback, as they collect data from standardized questioning rather than teacher reporting.
- **Video/audio recording:** When children participate in a performance task, audio or video recording can be very helpful for capturing student progress. Recordings can also allow families to view student behaviors with teachers and, later, provide parental interpretation and insight.
- **Anecdotal observations:** Teacher notes on student actions, or anecdotal observations, are a common way to collect data in early childhood. A record of only what teachers see and hear, an anecdotal observation shares an objective view of student learning.
- **Checklists:** Some teachers use checklists as a simple way to collect data. Because multiple school leaders can complete checklists on a child simultaneously, this documentation is a reliable way to track progress.
- **Frequency charts/graphs:** A frequency chart or graph can present a large amount of information easily. Additionally, frequency charts and graphs showcase trends and patterns in data efficiently.

- **Student projects:** Much like student work, student projects share examples of specific activities. Projects are useful to review with families because they often highlight specific student skill sets.
- **Interviewing:** In some cases, teachers may want to question students about their knowledge or behaviors. Hearing children's perspectives in their own words can be powerful evidence of learning.
- **Portfolios:** Portfolios are a collection of student work across a range of time. Portfolios are highly desirable in family-teacher conferencing because they share a variety of documentation sources.

Ideally, student documentation should be a part of every conference. As each type of documentation illustrates unique components of learning, teachers should incorporate several types. Further, creative forms of student documentation can intrigue and excite families, increasing their engagement in the conference. See the following table for some suggestions.

TYPES OF STUDENT DOCUMENTATION

Documentation Type	Examples
STUDENT WORK	• Student drawings • Letter/number writing • Writing samples • Math worksheets for older elementary children
PHOTOGRAPHS	• Students engaged in center activities, such as a child showing an understanding of addition with manipulatives • Completing classroom work • Using classroom resources or materials
ASSESSMENTS	• Spelling tests • Math quizzes • Evaluation reports • Developmental checklists • Teacher observational notes of children in play • Formative assessments

Documentation Type	Examples
VIDEO/AUDIO RECORDINGS	• Audio of oral reading • Recording of child explaining ways to make 5 from a group of blocks • Video of mealtime habits • Video of student performances, such as participation in a school sing-along
ANECDOTAL OBSERVATIONS	• Notes on student behaviors at nap time • Observations at playtime • Notes on social interaction with peers
CHECKLISTS	• Writing goals • Developmental milestones • Work habits, such as following directions
FREQUENCY CHARTS/GRAPHS	• Class participation • Sight word recognition • Physical aggression
STUDENT PROJECTS	• Art projects • Dioramas • Class presentations
INTERVIEWING	• School likes/dislikes • Steps used to solve a math problem • Learning challenges
PORTFOLIOS	• Subject-specific portfolios • Testing portfolio • Grade-level portfolios

Collecting Documentation

Purposeful instruction relates to effective documentation; one cannot happen without the other. Educators can only teach well when they have a sense of how their efforts shape student progress. Documentation keeps a record of this growth and, consequently, improves teaching practice and student engagement. Frequent assessment of student skills keeps teachers attentive to child needs, which helps in developing and revising appropriate interventions. This is why documentation should be a high priority for classroom teachers.

Nevertheless, teachers should not collect student work simply for the sake of having documentation. Instead, teacher efforts to document should always be intentional. Hilary Seitz (2008) suggests that teachers learn to document well through a series of stages.

- Teachers must learn what to document and identify appropriate collection methods.
- Teachers should figure out how important the documentation is for each student and define how to share that knowledge with parents and other stakeholders in meaningful ways.
- Teachers and families must partner to make relevant educational decisions.

MANAGING THE DOCUMENTATION PROCESS

Classrooms are active places, and documentation is an ongoing endeavor. Creating a manageable system is key to documenting student growth accurately and systematically. A good starting place is to devise a cycle of documenting student learning at regular intervals. For instance, a teacher may want to collect data every three weeks or at the close of a grading period. Alternatively, teachers may prefer to collect specific work samples at various points in the school year. As an example, a kindergarten teacher may gather handwriting samples from all students at the beginning, middle, and end of the school year.

Spontaneity—for observations in particular—is another way documentation can be more manageable for teachers. An unplanned observation occurs when a teacher takes advantage of an impromptu opportunity to engage with students. For example, while monitoring the classroom, a teacher may decide to observe as a child "reads" a picture book. Moments such as these may spark practical conversation between the teacher and the child, providing insights into social, communication, and comprehension skills. While scheduled data collection is useful for gathering information on targeted skills, an unplanned observation can remove some pressure around documentation for teachers, increasing the frequency of its use in the classroom.

Technology can be a useful resource for managing student documentation as well. Collecting data via video can capture student behaviors quickly. Further, digital portfolios make maintenance of student work simple for teachers while also increasing options for sharing data with multiple stakeholders. Students may be able to take the lead in documenting their own growth with tablets or digital cameras. These experiences also promote learning ownership, as students can select examples of their work to document and explain the reasoning for their choices.

DOCUMENTING FAIRLY AND ETHICALLY

Although documenting student growth is important, teachers should never prioritize documentation over students' well-being. Children have rights as learners that every teacher should honor. Classroom spaces should be safe learning environments. From the young child's perspective, the documentation process may feel uncomfortable. Children may not understand why their teachers are collecting their work or observing their play. Further, learning should be a joyful activity that promotes lifelong curiosity. Students should be able to experiment with concepts and ideas without fear that adults will record every error.

Ethical documentation finds an appropriate balance between student rights and teacher accountabilities. Monitoring student growth through multiple documentation efforts is a critical aspect of high-quality teaching. Data collection, however, is only one aspect of the teacher's role. First and foremost, the teachers have a responsibility to engage students. Early childhood educators set the foundation for how young children will view and understand the school experience. Effective teachers motivate students through their presence and interaction with them. Certainly, this dynamic changes when teachers are disproportionately invested in student documentation.

TIPS FOR DOCUMENTING FAIRLY AND ETHICALLY

- Secure permission to photograph or video students for the purpose of documenting their progress. State clearly how these materials will be used and shared within the learning community.
- Make every attempt to be unintrusive while observing students. Invasive observing can prevent students from behaving naturally.
- View each child as an individual. Teachers should recognize and respect each child's unique strengths and needs without comparing them to their peers.
- Use an objective approach in collecting data. Document student communication accurately without adding commentary or rationalizations.
- Remember that all documentation is a single moment in the child's learning. One incident or one assignment should not taint how teachers view or interpret future documentation.
- Be aware of personal biases. Teachers should be respectful of perspectives and ideas that are outside of their own experiences.
- Make every effort to maintain confidentiality. Teachers should never share identifiable student documentation among families or teachers with no connection to the child.

Collecting and interpreting student data also requires a fair and just perspective. Children are individuals, and as such, their performance should be interpreted through their unique characteristics rather than those of their peers. The teacher's own experiences and belief systems should remain separate from the documentation process; teachers must commit to regular reflections on their biases. Dependence on cultural beliefs can lead teachers to judge students and families unfairly. In contrast, teacher objectivity ensures that documentation is factual and accurate.

Sharing Student Documentation

The purpose of collecting documentation is to share it with people who can interpret it in meaningful ways. Families are especially skilled in this area, and consequently, their insight should be instrumental in educational planning and decision-making. How teachers present student documentation is often equally important as the information they share. Accordingly, teachers need a thoughtful approach to communicating documentation to families in conference meetings.

Sensitivity should be a paramount concern to teachers as they share documentation with families. While student data can sometimes feel very clinical and fact-based, the emotions families attach to their children are not. Regardless of the information, teachers should demonstrate empathy when discussing children with families. Similarly, teachers should be aware of any cultural beliefs that may influence how families receive or understand information.

Teachers should demonstrate respect for the students and families in their discussion of documentation. Teachers should remember that student documentation should present children's strengths as well as needs. Concerns illustrated via student data are not indicative of poor parenting, and documentation of student challenges should not label the child as deficient. In fact, messaging to families around student weaknesses should focus on how the teacher-family partnership can expand resources and support children's growth.

Finally, in the conference setting, teachers should take care to make data accessible to families. An overabundance of data can be overwhelming, making it difficult to process any documentation at all. Complex data collection systems or jargon can also hinder some families from comprehending documentation of their children's progress. Instead, a limited collection of compelling data explained in practical terms is most useful for engaging families.

Ms. June, a preschool teacher, presents an example of thoughtful documentation sharing. Ollie Miller is three years old and is transitioning from a day care to a preschool setting. While Ollie seems to be progressing well, Ms. Miller has requested a conference meeting to explore ideas for monitoring Ollie's academic development at home.

Ms. June studies her data on Ollie and selects several useful documentation options to share at the conference with Ms. Miller. First, she has observational notes from daily story time. Last week, Ollie recognized the letter O in "octopus" as a letter in his name. He also has begun to demonstrate an interest in story read-alouds, pointing to pictures and laughing at silly characters. Additionally, the teacher decides to show Ms. Miller photos of Ollie enjoying board books in the reading center, as well as a writing sample of Ollie printing the first letter of his name.

Sharing this documentation with Ms. Miller, Ms. June explains how each of these items is representative of Ollie's growing interest in reading and writing. He is beginning to recognize familiar letters and to comprehend stories that are read to him.

Ms. Miller is excited about this news and plans to read to Ollie each night to continue to develop his early literacy skills. Ms. June adds that it could be helpful to ask Ollie questions about the story characters and plot as the family reads together. She also recommends a few alphabet games and songs as a way to promote letter recognition.

Ms. June discussed Ollie's progress using documentation that was visual and interactive. Further, insight gained from the discussion of the materials was clear and actionable. Accordingly, the teacher and family could collaborate to support learning across home and school settings effectively.

Family Documentation

This chapter has focused on how teachers can use documentation to support the conference process. Families, too, may have useful data to share and discuss with teachers. In their interaction and observation of their children, families have unique perspectives on student progress. Experiences in the home and community can offer insight on behaviors and learning patterns. With this knowledge, teachers can broaden their understanding of children and families, improving their relationship building.

FAMILY PHOTOVOICE

In their 1997 article in the journal *Health, Education, and Behavior,* Caroline Wang and Mary Anne Burris discussed Photovoice as a means of collecting public health data. They described it as a way to enable people to document their community's strengths and challenges and to bring to light important issues through group discussion of photographs. Presently, Photovoice is a common research method for sharing personal perspective through photography.

In schools, teachers can encourage families to use the Photovoice approach to illustrate home and community influences on their child's development. With the use of photographs, families can document, and later discuss with teachers, their child's learning processes.

Many families may not readily recognize the significant effect small efforts can have on student achievement. The Photovoice method provides families with the opportunity to share photos of useful strategies or resources that support their child's learning strengths.

In some circumstances, Photovoice showcases barriers that impede student progress, such as insufficient supplies or inappropriate resources. Such knowledge may enhance teacher advocacy for schoolwide or community policy change.

Family documentation can be a more naturalistic approach to learning from children. Although often less formal than school data, families can use many of the same types of documentation that teachers use to showcase progress, including photographs, audio/video, and student work. In their day-to-day activities, families can serve as familiar observers to their children. Coupled with a safe environment and limited distractions, family documentation can illustrate potential supports or scaffolding that teachers can apply in the classroom.

Nonetheless, teachers should use family documentation as an addition to, rather than a substitute for, school-based data. Teachers should be concerned with not only studying student products but also the process. In the classroom, teachers can confirm the structure and rigor of assignments and expectations. The child's level of independence, for example, may not be described in family documentation. This information is key to understanding how skills can be replicated or applied to new situations.

Mr. and Mrs. Wallace had some concerns about the attention span of their four-year-old daughter, Emma. At home, Emma seemed to move from activity to activity, failing to complete tasks. Emma's teacher, Mr. Dylan, had concerns as well. In fact, he met with the family several times during the month to share concerns about Emma's struggles to focus during circle and story time.

During a recent phone conference with the family, Mr. Dylan suggested that Mr. and Mrs. Wallace keep a simple observation journal at home to examine Emma's behaviors more closely. In a small notebook, the family recorded Emma's activities and behaviors, and their responses as parents. At the end of two weeks, the Wallace family reviewed the information they captured.

The family discovered two interesting patterns. First, Emma enjoys creative projects. When Emma was engaged in art, music, or dance activities, she stayed focused for almost ten minutes without breaks. Second, Emma persisted longer at tasks when she worked for a reward, such as a sticker or small candy. Emma also thrived on her parents' positive praise.

The next week, the family met with Mr. Dylan via video conference to review the journal and discuss key observations. They explained Emma's interests, challenges, and successful strategies used at home. The family and Mr. Dylan explored ways that school staff can use the family's documentation to support Emma at school.

Throughout the following month, Mr. Dylan integrated music, songs, and fingerplays in classroom lessons. He also used a behavior chart to motivate Emma to sit quietly with still hands during story and circle time. Emma enjoyed earning stickers that she could exchange for small prizes and treats. In the first week, Emma made good progress with her attention skills.

Families are experts in their children's strengths, needs, and preferences. Documenting this knowledge can help families articulate their insight in a meaningful way. In this case, the Wallace family shared observations of their child that shaped useful classroom interventions. This exchange of information also empowers the family to continue to actively participate in their child's education.

How to Use the Family-Teacher Conference Documentation Gathering Tool

Documentation improves the messaging in family-teacher conferences by providing visual representation of abstract learning goals. Effective communication increases productivity in conferencing, enhancing understanding for teachers and families. With clear evidence of student progress at hand, teachers and families can focus on celebrating student achievements or problem-solving concerns. Additionally, documentation creates awareness of learning expectations for students.

The Family-Teacher Conference Documentation Gathering Tool helps teachers organize documentation for conferences. Designed to stimulate conversation about student strengths and needs, the tool is divided into two sections, one for recognizing student growth and another for highlighting concerns. The teacher begins by talking with family about the student's strengths, then uses the checklist to indicate the documentation they will have gathered to highlight this progress. After sharing the documentation of strengths, the teacher repeats the process, acknowledging a student concern. The tool also includes a space for writing key insights from the documentation and for recording questions or concerns from the family.

Although helpful for preparing in the days before individual conferencing meetings, this tool has value several weeks ahead of family meetings too. During this timeframe, teachers may reflect on the appropriate documentation to collect to best illustrate student progress. Further, this approach gives teachers time to explore and gather data on effective interventions to support or sustain skills.

Documentation is a useful way to share students' strengths and needs with families. Student data, in all its many forms, provides families with clear evidence of progress, maintenance, and regression. When teachers are intentional in their integration of documentation in the conference setting, families learn to interpret student performance effectively, equipping them to better support their children's learning. Chapter 6 will discuss how to partner with families when documentation indicates persistent academic, behavioral, or social student concerns.

FAMILY-TEACHER CONFERENCE DOCUMENTATION GATHERING TOOL

Student Name ____________________ **Conference Date** ____________

Student Strengths

____

____

Student Growth: Documentation Prepared

- ☐ Student Work/Projects
- ☐ Photos
- ☐ Assessments
- ☐ Tests
- ☐ Video/Audio
- ☐ Checklists
- ☐ Frequency Charts
- ☐ Interviews
- ☐ Portfolios

Notes:

Student Challenges

____

____

Student Concerns: Documentation Prepared

- ☐ Student Work/Projects
- ☐ Photos
- ☐ Assessments
- ☐ Tests
- ☐ Video/Audio
- ☐ Checklists
- ☐ Frequency Charts
- ☐ Interviews
- ☐ Portfolios

Notes:

Key Insights from Documentation

Questions and Follow-Up Concerns

CHAPTER 6

PARTNERING FOR PROBLEM SOLVING

"Even on his worst day, my child is still a good kid."

—PARENT OF PRE-K STUDENT

At its core, school is a place of significant development for students. Each day, the classroom setting provides children with a variety of learning opportunities. Learning, however, is rarely a linear process. Mistakes are always a part of it, as are setbacks and regression. All students will encounter challenges in the classroom at some point in their school career. With self-reflection and teacher guidance, some students can navigate these difficulties effortlessly. For others, the pathway to success can be far more complicated.

A wide assortment of concerns, both individually and collectively, can induce learning challenges for children. Obstacles can span over and across all development domains, including academic, social, and behavioral. For example, a child who is struggling to read might be teased by her peers, triggering her to bite a classmate. Personal experiences can also prompt how students respond in the classroom. Stressors or changes in the school or home environments can shape student behaviors significantly. Past or present trauma can make it difficult for students to focus on learning expectations. Undiagnosed learning needs can lead to ongoing concerns as well.

Yet, as expressed in the introductory family quote, all children have inherent merit, regardless of their learning challenges. The concerns that a child faces today are not predictive of their present value or future achievement. A child who misreads sight words, breaks crayons in the art center, or repeatedly interrupts during story time is still deserving of teacher care and respect. This is why teachers must take frequent inventory of their students' strengths and talents. Staying conscious of their positive contributions to the learning community is a useful reminder of the limitless potential of students. Such knowledge should serve as motivation for teachers to persist in helping students to navigate learning concerns successfully.

Even with teacher redirection and support, some struggles will develop into significant challenges for students. In these cases, teachers must explore more intensive interventions. Partnering with families should always be a teacher's first step toward supporting the child. Through a collaborative approach, both teachers and families can use their expertise to contribute to a reasonable action plan. While the teacher's professional background provides developmental guidance, the family can offer child-specific knowledge that can enhance the effectiveness of classroom strategies.

Accordingly, teachers must prioritize communicating student learning concerns with families. Ignoring the problem or accepting it as standard practice does little to improve outcomes. Both teachers and families should have important roles in developing an appropriate action plan for addressing student concerns. When teachers describe student needs with a balance of sensitivity and accuracy, families can accept accountability in their child's progress. A strong partnership better equips teachers and families to make informed decisions about the child's education.

Understanding Student Concerns

Teaching in contemporary society is a tremendously complicated process. Early childhood teachers cannot simply lecture content and expect their students to grasp the material. Instead, teachers must know the children individually, incorporating their interests and preferences into instructional practices. Additionally, children's retention of ideas is dependent on teachers incorporating a variety of learning styles into their daily lessons. Through these means, teachers can create and sustain student engagement in the classroom.

However, even when teachers have effective methods, students can still struggle to make significant progress. Although the surrounding community may prioritize academics, teachers must monitor the growth of the whole child–the social-emotional, physical, and behavioral development of students alongside their cognitive achievements. In observing young children in the classroom, teachers will discover that students rarely progress uniformly. At times, students may be more advanced in one developmental area while showing deficits in another. When these gaps are significant and persistent, student concerns result.

ACADEMIC STUDENT CONCERNS

Academic concerns occur from time to time for all students. Students may struggle to understand material, making it difficult for them to proceed in their learning. In some cases, academic student concerns can be directly related to understanding, interpreting, or manipulating the content. For instance, a kindergarten child may have difficulty writing, recognizing, comparing, or ordering numbers. Academic concerns can also be related to receiving, processing, or retrieving information. In this case, the kindergarten student would struggle with numeracy because of difficulty focusing, storing, organizing, or applying the information.

SOCIAL-EMOTIONAL CONCERNS

Schools provide students with many opportunities to practice social skills. For young children especially, transitioning from a home environment to a classroom where they must share the attention of a single teacher with several classmates can be very difficult. Social-emotional student concerns can center on self-management skills, such as emotional regulation, following directions, or communicating needs. Engaging with other children can also pose a challenge. Some children may struggle with sharing, showing empathy, or resolving conflict.

MENTAL HEALTH IN EARLY CHILDHOOD

Like physical well-being, mental health is crucial to children's success in school. Children who are mentally healthy are better able to focus on learning, build supportive relationships, and manage their emotional needs. The Centers for Disease Control and Prevention (2023) report that about 17 percent of children ages two to eight years have a mental, behavioral, or developmental disorder. Common childhood mental health disorders for this age group include attention deficit, anxiety, and behavior disorders.

In many cases, these mental health disorders prompt or intensify student concerns within the classroom. A safe and structured classroom creates a favorable environment for navigating persistent stressors. Additionally, partnering with teachers may help to connect struggling children and families with appropriate supports and services.

BEHAVIORAL CONCERNS

At times, the classroom environment can feel overwhelming to young children. When they are confronted with stressful or frustrating circumstances, children may respond undesirably to obtain a specific goal. Whether negative, positive, or neutral, all behavior communicates children's responses to the world around them. Challenging behaviors reveal feelings about preferences, dislikes, and needs. For instance, a child who hides under a table during playtime may do so to share the desire for more drawing time, disinterest in engaging with peers, or the need for a quiet space. Thoughtfully studying student problem behaviors in this way can determine their function within the classroom. With this knowledge, educators can support student needs and shape behaviors appropriately. The following table lists some common examples of academic, social-emotional, and behavioral student concerns.

ACADEMIC CONCERNS	SOCIAL-EMOTIONAL CONCERNS	BEHAVIORAL CONCERNS
• Misunderstanding the content • Content disinterest • Disorganization • Procrastination • Absenteeism • Inattentiveness • Learning disabilities	• Impulsivity • Separation from peers • Anxiety • Communication issues • Emotional dysregulation • Inflexibility	• Physical aggression • Bullying • Defiance • Disrespect • Temper tantrums • Toileting issues • Self-injury, such as finger picking, hitting self, and so on

Discussing Student Concerns with Families

Discussing student concerns with families can feel incredibly awkward for parents and teachers. Certainly, it is much more enjoyable to highlight student growth rather than areas of struggle. However, open communication about student needs can increase teacher efforts in the classroom. Working with families expands teacher knowledge and resources to support children and can also accelerate the timeline to success. Family insight can provide constructive feedback on interventions that may otherwise delay student progress. Perhaps most importantly, collaborating with families to address student concerns strengthens the relationship between teachers and families, renewing their collective commitment to student progress.

Nonetheless, problem solving with families requires some finesse on the teacher's part. Teachers who discuss student concerns with anger or disgust can alienate families from the start, prompting a defensive response. A conference agenda that only addresses student shortcomings can discourage families from working toward a solution. Neither of these responses sets the tone for successful conferencing.

PROBLEM SOLVING DURING FAMILY-TEACHER CONFERENCES

Because each parent is different, teachers should use a variety of strategies to partner with families. In particular, productive problem solving must build a genuine sense of agency among families. In this way, families can contribute to decision-making within the conference problem-solving process. Although they still may be reluctant to engage initially, creating a space for families to ask questions, seek clarification, and provide ongoing feedback is crucial to collaborative problem solving. Teachers can use the following steps to solicit active participation from families:

- **Share information.** Problem solving must begin with information sharing. Teachers should discuss the concern clearly and directly. Whenever possible, the teacher should offer details about the concern along with how the teacher has addressed the concern to date. Using examples and/or documentation is a useful way to demonstrate the impact of the concern on student progress. It can also be helpful to share how the discussed behavior falls outside of developmentally appropriate expectations for the student's age.

- **Solicit insight.** Once the teacher has identified the student concern, the educator should ask for the family's insight. In particular, the teacher may be interested to know how the family addresses the behavior in the home setting or how events in the child's life may have influenced their progress.

- **Seek support.** When both teachers and families have a good understanding of student concerns and possible antecedents, they can then discuss how to support student progress appropriately. Families may offer suggestions for motivating, guiding, or rewarding their children. Teachers and families could also explore supports that promote learning in the home setting.

- **Review the discussion.** Conclude the problem-solving segment of the conference with a review of major discussion points. Highlight student goals, discuss teacher and family support efforts, and set a timeline for monitoring student progress.

Problem solving within conference settings takes committed practice. Teachers must listen carefully to families and embrace their insight and expertise. A simple or easy solution is not always possible, and families sometimes need guidance on developing a practical action plan for the classroom. However, when teachers and families agree to persist in their support, children can progress over time. The following chart shares sample teacher language for conference problem solving.

SAMPLE LANGUAGE FOR CONFERENCE PROBLEM SOLVING

Share Information

"For two weeks, I noticed that Angel has been struggling to stay focused during independent work time. I tried breaking the assignments into smaller tasks and providing her with a quiet area to work. These strategies have helped only minimally."

↓

Solicit Insight

"Does this behavior sound familiar to anything you have observed at home? Have you noticed any similar behaviors when you give Angel directions or ask her to help with chores at home? How quickly does she complete tasks independently?"

↓

Seek Support

"How might I better support Angel in the classroom? Do you have ideas for rewards that could motivate her? Are there other people at home or school who may have useful recommendations for us?"

↓

Review the Discussion

"I am glad that we agree that Angel needs to improve her independent work habits. We have a solid plan for moving forward. I will do [agreed upon intervention] at school, and you will do [agreed upon intervention] at home. Let's plan to meet again next week to discuss progress."

When Children May Need More Support

Navigating student concerns is an important part of healthy development. As children persist in challenges, they gain skills that they can apply to new situations. However, children who have consistent and significant academic, behavioral, or social concerns may raise more questions for teachers. Even with effective interventions and strong family partnerships, some children will continue to struggle to make progress. In these instances, they may need more support than teachers can provide in the general education classroom. Ongoing learning challenges may prompt teachers to broach the topic of evaluating a student for a learning or developmental disability.

Discussing the potential of a disability in the conference setting is never a simple endeavor. For most families, when their child's teacher shares concerns about their child's development, the suggestion can be very difficult to process. With only their own child as a measure, some families may fail to see how enduring struggles are affecting their child's progress. In these cases, a teacher recommendation for a professional evaluation can leave family members feeling stunned and overwhelmed. In response, some families may counter with anger and resistance.

Consequently, it is crucial that teachers demonstrate sensitivity to the families' feelings when making a recommendation for a disability evaluation. Hearing that their child may have a disability may rouse feelings of shame, anger, depression, or frustration. Similarly, families may fear how a potential disability may affect their child's future. Teachers can show empathy in these situations by providing families with the time and space to process their feelings. It is also important that teachers reassure families that they remain committed to the student's progress regardless of whether the family decides to pursue an evaluation.

Ms. Paige has scheduled a conference with Mr. and Mrs. Hernandez, the parents of Jacki, a bright and curious four-year-old. Ms. Paige begins the conference by sharing how much she enjoys having Jacki in class. Jacki can already identify many sight words and is reading simple books in the classroom library. Yet she has some challenges as well. During center play, Jacki refuses to play with any other toys besides the alphabet blocks and responds to her name infrequently. She is also still struggling to communicate her needs and wants, and she engages in several repetitive motions, such as spinning in a circle and bumping her body into walls. Given these ongoing concerns, Ms. Paige suggests that a developmental evaluation may be useful to tailor appropriate support for Jacki in the classroom. Although Ms. Paige and the Hernandez family have discussed Jacki's challenges previously, the parents' faces still register disappointment and anxiety.

Ms. Paige is mindful of the family's response. She reiterates that a developmental evaluation will provide valuable data that will inform decisions that the team–the teacher, family, and student–can make together to help Jacki experience greater success in the classroom. Following, Ms. Paige pauses and solicits questions from Mr. and Mrs. Hernandez. The teacher provides gentle but honest responses to the

family's concerns. Ms. Paige assures the family that she will continue to partner with them to adapt activities for Jacki. As the conference ends, Ms. Paige offers details about the evaluation procedures and how the family pediatrician can support the evaluation process. While still processing the information Ms. Paige shared, the Hernandez family is grateful for her open and clear communication about their daughter's progress. Now, they have a better understanding of how an evaluation can help, rather than hurt, their child's education.

As illustrated in this example, discussions about disability evaluations can be productive and useful to teachers and families alike. Although recommending a student for disability testing is never pleasant or easy, a sensitive disposition can sustain a positive family-teacher relationship and enhance collaborative interaction.

TIPS FOR DISCUSSING SUSPICION OF DISABILITY IN CONFERENCE SETTINGS

- **Demonstrate patience.** Families may need time to consider a recommendation for an evaluation thoughtfully. Do not pressure families to make a decision about seeking an evaluation immediately.
- **Be knowledgeable about the evaluation process.** Review potential next steps with families as well as their role in providing consent, student information, and other documentation. Temper expectations appropriately; remember, the evaluation process can take several months to conduct. Discuss how the child will continue to receive support in the classroom in the meantime.
- **Avoid labeling the child with a specific disability.** Disabilities can manifest differently in children, and teachers are not trained to diagnose students.
- **Encourage families to seek an evaluation first to gather additional insight on the child's strengths and needs.** This information can assist teachers and families in making informed decisions.

Using Conflict Resolution

Teachers and families will not always agree during conferences, and disagreements that cannot be resolved quickly can result in conflict. Although it can be uncomfortable, conflict can prompt teachers to examine their biases and consider new perspectives. Conversely, when teachers and families refuse to compromise, they impair the productivity of the conference. Additionally, ongoing conflict can damage the family-teacher relationship. Families are far less likely to trust teachers when they feel unheard.

Mitigating conflict in the conference setting requires teachers to be reflective. Given the short timeframe of the conference, it may not be possible for teachers to have a deep consideration of the family's point of view. Nonetheless, it is critical that teachers attempt to understand the family's concerns and identify a way to move forward in problem solving. Often, this means that teachers must prioritize their role as active listeners over their desire to lead the conversation. Other efforts to resolve conflict in the conference setting, such as those in the following list, should demonstrate empathy and understanding.

- **Set clear expectations.** Before discussing student concerns, articulate the expected outcomes for the discussion. All stakeholders should be aware of the goals of the conversation.

- **Acknowledge emotions.** If discussions become heated, emotions may become heightened as well. Teachers should monitor the family's response as well as their own. If it appears that either the family member or teacher cannot manage their emotions, the teacher should suggest reconvening the discussion at another time.

- **Stress positive intentions.** The best interests of the child should always be at the center of the teacher's actions. Teachers should clearly communicate how their recommendations will support the student and the family.

- **Compromise.** Neither teachers nor families achieve every desired outcome in a conference. Both parties should seek common ground in problem solving. Then, teachers and families can identify strategies, resources, and systems that best support the child's progress.

- **Offer choice.** Similar to students, families appreciate having choices as participants in their children's education. Rather than dictating what parents should do to support their children, teachers should listen to family concerns and then provide reasonable options that meet student and family needs. See the Problem Solving through Choice Reflection Tool as one teacher strategy for exploring family preferences in decision-making

- **Collaborate with colleagues.** Soliciting the insight or support of colleagues can help teachers remain present in the conversation. A school principal, center director, or trusted teacher can mediate a difficult situation and negotiate conflict effectively.

- **Stay focused.** At times, families advocate for their children in unlikable ways. Avoid taking criticism personally. Instead, revisit the goals of discussion and encourage the family to focus on ways to support the child.

How to Use the Problem Solving through Choice Reflection Tool

Offering families choices is one of the best ways to promote family-led problem solving and decision-making. A sense of agency empowers families to assume an active role in school conferencing. Choice also assigns a sense of accountability to families, increasing their commitment to the action plan. Providing families with options to solve problems helps them to visualize the concern more completely and to better understand the logistics of their options. Collectively, this knowledge helps families make sound choices about their children's education.

The process of problem solving through choice has three steps:

- First, teachers must listen thoughtfully to the family's point of view.

- Second, the teacher must provide their perspective, stressing how the discussed issue will affect the child's progress and well-being.

- Finally, given the concern, the teacher must offer two or more practical and reasonable choices to support the child and family.

The family can then move forward with choosing the option that they believe will benefit their child most.

The following Problem Solving through Choice Reflection Tool gives teachers practice identifying and providing choices to families. The initial example scenario shares a teacher's perspective and family choice options. The second and third practice scenarios present two different concerns in need of the teacher's perspective and family choice options, respectively. The final practice exercise prompts teachers to reflect on how they might use this technique to address a family concern that they may encounter in an upcoming conference.

All students encounter challenges in their school careers. Communicating with families is essential for addressing concerns. Further, teachers and families must accept their role in supporting student progress. When teachers and families join expertise and resources, students have the best opportunity to overcome barriers to learning. Yet, just as all students face struggles, all learners have assets, too. Chapter 7 highlights how to acknowledge and celebrate achievements in the conference setting.

PROBLEM SOLVING THROUGH CHOICE REFLECTION TOOL

Example scenario:

Family: "I don't want my child enrolled in the math readiness program."

Teacher: "The math readiness program provides intensive, small-group reinforcement of foundational number skills. However, working one-on-one with your child at home, seeking an outside tutoring service, and continuing our current classroom supports are all good options, too. As the child's parent, you know his capabilities best."

Practice scenario: Add choices

Family: "There's no way I can find the time to read to my child every night."

Teacher: "Reading at home builds literacy skills and strengthens vocabulary development, but at present, it is not a required home-learning assignment."

What choices might the teacher provide for this family with respect to this concern?

____

____

____

Practice scenario: Add the teacher's perspective

Family: "I don't want my daughter to take a nap in kindergarten."

Teacher: "Students can recharge for the afternoon in many ways. Would you prefer to have your child read books quietly or l sten to music with headphones during rest time?"

What might be the teacher's perspective on this family concern?

____

____

____

Teacher-suggested scenario

What family opinion might be brought up at the next school conference? How will you stress your perspective but provide the family with reasonable options for meeting the child's needs?

Family: ____

____

Teacher: ____

____

____

CHAPTER 7

CELEBRATING ACHIEVEMENTS

"I always knew my kid was special, but it meant a lot to know that the teacher believed it too."

—PARENT OF THIRD-GRADE STUDENT

Family-teacher conferences can have a bad reputation. Given television and movie portrayals of school conferencing, this attitude is hardly a surprise. Rarely do these fictional interactions reflect communication patterns featuring collaborative problem solving. Instead, the typical storyline depicts a disruptive school incident as the prompt for a teacher-led discussion where teachers itemize children's faults and point blame at families. Unsurprisingly, in this scenario, neither the teacher nor the family leave the conversation feeling hopeful or supported. This view of family-teacher conferencing only serves to damage the relationship among teachers, families, and students.

Students go to school to learn, and making mistakes is part of the learning process. Partnering with families supports children as they gain and practice skills. While urgent concerns will require an immediate conference with families, celebrating student success should be a part of every school meeting. This is not to suggest, however, that every aspect of the school conference will be positive or easy for families to hear.

Nonetheless, every child, regardless of their background, has strengths, and building on these assets should serve as motivation for effective conferencing. A whole-child approach honors and nurtures the collection of academic, social, and behavioral gifts that children bring to the classroom. During conferences, teachers should be diligent about celebrating student progress in a variety of learning situations. In this way, teachers send a clear message to families that they see the child as more than a test score, a letter grade, or a behavioral issue.

As children's caregivers, many families are highly skilled at recognizing their child's strengths. However, families of children who struggle with problem behaviors or academic achievement may not be accustomed to teachers celebrating their child. As the quote at the beginning of this chapter suggests, families appreciate and find comfort in positive messaging from teachers. Teachers who celebrate students' achievements affirm the parents' own positive feelings about their children, and by extension, affirm parenting roles as well.

Acknowledging student successes during school conferences develops a positive bond between the family and the teacher.

Families are more willing to discuss student challenges when they know that the teacher recognizes potential in the student. Success sharing accomplishes much more than simply recognizing students' talents. This action communicates high expectations and sends a message that the teacher believes in the inherent abilities of the child. In short, highlighting student achievements generates feelings of hope for future progress. For both families and teachers, hope serves as a powerful stimulus for collaborative family-teacher partnerships.

Celebrating Student Achievements

Everyone appreciates good news. For many parents, hearing about their child's successes is among the best news they can receive. Families cherish outside confirmation that their children are developing and making progress. Within the family-teacher conference, however, celebrating student achievements holds an even more significant purpose. Beginning the conference with stories of students' strengths sets a positive tone for the meeting and stimulates active participation in the conference among families. Alternatively, starting the conference with student deficits can place families immediately on the defense, stifling productive engagement for the remainder of the conference.

Additionally, a positive start to the conference can ease the family's apprehension or anxiety about the conference. Remember that some families have uncomfortable feelings toward the school environment. Their only interaction with the school before the conference may have been unpleasant or stressful. A positive comment may be sufficient to change the narrative around the family-teacher relationship for some parents, encouraging supportive partnering.

BENEFITS OF CELEBRATING STUDENT ACHIEVEMENTS

Celebrating student achievements during the family-teacher conference has value beyond the school meeting. All direct stakeholders—families, teachers, and children—will reap the benefits when teachers acknowledge student success during conferencing. With some teacher facilitation and guidance, educators and families can leave the meeting with knowledge to better support their efforts and those of the children. In this way, students can continue to make progress in the classroom.

Unlike teachers, families do not have the privilege of being a regular part of the daily classroom environment. As such, they often do not have an opportunity to witness student progress as it unfolds through school activities. Sharing successes gives families a glimpse of their child's growth with respect to age-appropriate goals and milestones, providing feedback on their support of student learning outside of school. Even small achievements can serve as the encouragement families need to persist with their efforts, especially when student gains have required constant and demanding endeavors.

When families share student successes with their children, the students benefit as well. Many young children want to please the special adults in their lives. Knowing that their behaviors have delighted their teacher and family, many children will want to work hard to continue the behavior. Most importantly, by reflecting on their own feelings of pride, self-worth, and achievement, students can gain the self-motivation to repeat the behavior for themselves. When students revisit past successes, they build resilience for tackling new tasks.

Much like families and students, teachers need encouragement to persist as well. As teachers celebrate student successes, they cannot help but recognize their own. Through thoughtful planning and reflective practices, teachers have a significant role in developing student skills. These gains are added to the teacher's repertoire to build an effective practice that creates professional competence. Positive messages about students build rapport with families, increasing the likelihood that they will share insight, ideas, or resources with the teacher.

Crafting Meaningful, Positive Messages

Celebrating achievements is more than stating basic facts about the child. Although the "sandwich model"—using positive comments before and after stating concerns—is a useful framework for beginning and ending a conference constructively, teachers should avoid sharing uniform student strengths with every parent. Acknowledging student achievements is not a conference obligation to be checked off a planning list. Instead, to carry meaning for families, teachers should use positive messages that authentically highlight individual child strengths.

Positive messages about students have several qualities. They should be timely, specific, and intentional. First, positive messages should be timely. Teachers should share comments about student progress and skill development while children are still exhibiting that growth in daily routines and activities. It is of no use to share comments with families about skills that have long been established or are no longer present. Timely celebrations allow families to reflect on their current parenting choices that may have influenced student success and to reinforce appropriate goals with their children.

Positive messages in conference settings should also be specific. Clearly communicated, well-crafted positive messages should provide critical details on student behaviors. Families take pride in comments that the teacher describes with unique child-specific details. Further, a rich description of student strengths told through a classroom anecdote will surely be more memorable for a family than a general statement or a checklist of skill sets. Families are much more likely to share and celebrate these messages with their children, creating a higher probability for the behavior to continue.

Positive messages should carry a purpose for the teacher and the families. Teachers should be intentional about the messages they share with families. Positive messages should supply feedback on not only the behavior itself but also what the behavior indicates about the child's progress. Such a discussion gives families insight into developmentally appropriate behaviors, highlighting areas where the student is meeting or exceeding expectations. Such information is useful for monitoring, supporting, and enhancing behavior in home and community settings.

Mr. James is meeting with Ms. Grayson about her son, Alec, a kindergarten student in his classroom. The first month of school has been a smooth transition for Alec. He has made many friends and is progressing well in all subjects. Mr. James wants to share a positive message about Alec at the onset of the conference that will illustrate his successful kindergarten placement. An exchange with Alec last week immediately comes to mind. Prompted by the photographs in a nonfiction book, Alec raised his hand to share information about the life cycle of butterflies. In his description, Alec correctly used scientific terminology, such as *larva* and *chrysalis*. Upon reflection, Mr. James realizes that Alec frequently demonstrates complex knowledge in many

different areas. Further, Alec is a quick learner, grasping and retaining concepts with little repetition.

As the conference opens, Mr. James shares the butterfly story. Ms. Grayson is proud but unsurprised by the anecdote. She notes that Alec has always had a strong memory and is keenly interested in how things in the world work. Mr. James explains how Alec's sophisticated vocabulary, memory, and curiosity are all signs of advanced maturity in kindergarten students.

Mr. James highlights how he supports Alec in the classroom by promoting independence and creativity in class assignments. Then, he offers some suggestions of how Ms. Grayson might cultivate Alec's skills in the home setting. He recommends encouraging Alec to explore topics of interest as well as offering stimulating activities, such as puzzles and science kits. Ms. Grayson adds to the conversation by proposing trips to the local library and the art museum.

Positive messages have the power to be much more than empty praise. In this example, the teacher used positive messaging to communicate specific skills. When viewed as evidence of student progress or potential, teachers and families can work together to enhance student growth and learning.

TIPS FOR DEVELOPING POSITIVE MESSAGES FOR CONFERENCING

- Prior to each conference meeting, reflect on the student's strengths. Consider specific examples of the child's talents in action within the classroom, and share personal stories that illustrate their child's practical skill use.
- Share student work and materials to show, rather than tell about, student successes. Collect student work in a portfolio so that families can review progress throughout a grading period and across content areas. Use photos or videos to share growth in social or behavioral skills with families.
- Acknowledge the family's role in student achievement. A child's success is often a testament to the family's investment in their child's progress. Urge families to share how they have reinforced skill development within the home. Thank families for their support.
- If the conference is moving in the wrong direction, do not be afraid to ask to restart the meeting. Clearly restate the purpose of the meeting and begin with another positive message about the child.

BARRIERS TO POSITIVE MESSAGES

While positive messages are always useful, logistical and situational challenges can make it more difficult for teachers to share these messages with families. Time constraints can pressure teachers to move quickly through a script of conference highlights. From the teacher's perspective, structuring a flexible conference schedule that includes ample time to address the needs of all stakeholders is an easy solution to this concern. Families' availability, however, may be more limited. In these cases, it is to the teacher's advantage to develop direct yet powerful messages to connect with families about their children's strengths.

Significant academic or behavioral concerns represent another potential barrier to positive message sharing. When teachers are faced with urgent classroom issues, they may delve directly into student challenges from the beginning of the conference. Such an approach can antagonize and alienate families, making it difficult to problem solve or collaborate effectively. Similarly, families may join the conference feeling emotional, making it more difficult for teachers to set the stage for positive interaction of any kind. Under these circumstances, teachers will need to persist in weaving student achievements into the conference discussion.

Mr. Graham has been invited to a conference to discuss concerns about Colin, his four-year-old son. Colin struggles with transitioning from center activities in the classroom. In particular, he often screams and tantrums when he is asked to move from the block center. Recently, Colin's behaviors have escalated aggressively, including kicking and hitting. Colin's teacher, Miss Stacey, has provided frequent communication and regular updates on progress with the family.

Although Miss Stacey has made it clear that she wants to partner with Mr. Graham to help Colin, Mr. Graham enters the conference visibly upset and anxious. He is confident this conference is meant to discuss Colin's removal from the school program. Miss Stacey attempts to begin the conference with a positive message, but Mr. Graham insists he wants the teacher to "give it to him straight" and not to "sugarcoat" Colin's problems. Nonetheless, Miss Stacey insists on showing Mr. Graham digital photographs of one of Colin's most impressive block-building projects. She highlights his advanced fine motor and creative designing skills. She follows the photographs with an anecdote about how Colin invited a shy, new student to play with him during the child's first day in the classroom.

Miss Stacey watches as the tension on Mr. Graham's face slowly begins to fade. Mr. Graham chimes in to share how he and Colin enjoy building block models at home and how he has taught Colin to persist with challenging building projects. Miss Stacey highlights a few of the benefits of this father-son time and thanks Mr. Graham for supporting learning experiences in the home. Miss Stacey expresses that she hopes that they can continue to collaborate to help Colin manage his behaviors in the classroom. Mr. Graham suggests an idea for a reward chart for Colin that can be used to shape positive behaviors at school and home.

Barriers to positive messaging will always be present in the classroom. Miss Stacey could have easily begun the conversation with the child's struggles, citing the parent's seemingly limited time or the significance of the concern as the motivation for this decision. However, this choice would have most definitely intensified Mr. Graham's worrisome feelings, inhibiting useful family engagement. Instead, Miss Stacey's commitment to celebrating Colin's strengths set the conference on a pathway of productive conversation and problem-solving.

REFRAMING CHALLENGING BEHAVIORS

Teachers must be focused on seeing the positive in every student. Admittedly, this task may be easier for teachers to accomplish with some students than others. Challenging behaviors, even persistent ones, do not determine a child's value or future capabilities. One of the best ways to communicate this idea to families is through underscoring strong skill sets within behavior concerns. In no way does this suggest that teachers should glorify poor student choices or ignore disruptive or unsafe behaviors. Instead, the purpose of this approach is to remind teachers and families of the inherent potential within every child. Teachers and families can then use this information as a foundation for goal setting around shaping appropriate, functional skill sets. The following table provides some examples of how teachers can reframe challenging behaviors and work with families to reinforce functionally appropriate skills.

REFRAMING CHALLENGING STUDENT BEHAVIORS

Challenging Behavior	Reframed Behavior	Teacher Reinforcement of Appropriate Behavior	Family Reinforcement of Appropriate Behavior
Student yells out answers during math class.	**The student is excelling in math. She can articulate her understanding and share her ideas with peers.**	**The teacher will praise the student each time she raises her hand and waits to be called on in class.**	**The family will practice turn-taking with the student at home through natural activities, such as playing games, conversation, sharing toys, and so on.**

Challenging Behavior	Reframed Behavior	Teacher Reinforcement of Appropriate Behavior	Family Reinforcement of Appropriate Behavior
Student hides under a table during large-group time.	The student is aware of his wants and needs. He has identified places of comfort in the classroom.	The teacher will provide the student with an opportunity to ask for a break during large-group time. The teacher will give the child three minutes in a safe, comfortable place in the classroom before encouraging him to return to the group.	The family will give the child small breaks during nonpreferred tasks, such as clearing the table after dinner. Following the break, the family will hold the child accountable to returning to the task.
Student makes peers laugh by making silly faces in class.	The student has a good sense of humor. She is a leader among her peers in the classroom.	The teacher will offer the student a leadership role in the class, such as a classroom job, peer helper, and so on.	The family will assign one or two new, developmentally appropriate responsibilities at home, such as simple chores. The family will offer the child choice in selecting these new responsibilities.
Student draws pictures of animals on his school desk.	The student has artistic interest and talent. He enjoys sharing his work with others.	The teacher will allow the student to earn special paper or drawing materials when he draws on appropriate surfaces.	The family will expose the child to drawing/ art activities online or within the community.

THEMES FOR POSITIVE MESSAGES ABOUT CHILDREN

Children have many wonderful ways of being. A whole-child approach embraces many aspects of the child's progress across several developmental domains. By exploring a variety of themes, teachers can model for families an appreciation of the multitude of skills and talents within each child. In this way, families can collaborate with teachers to nurture child-specific skill sets.

CELEBRATING A GROWTH MINDSET

In 2006, Carol Dweck wrote about the concept of a growth mindset in her book *Mindset: The New Psychology of Success.* A growth mindset refers to a person's belief that time and effort can produce significant achievement. Conversely, a fixed mindset accepts a static view of intelligence and ability.

Proponents of growth mindset theory recommend that teachers discuss, model, and implement growth mindset strategies in the classroom early and often. Children as young as toddlers can develop and exhibit growth mindset skill sets.

Early childhood teachers should keep a watchful eye for growth mindset language and behaviors in their classroom and share development in this area with families. A growth mindset prepares students to take risks, work hard, and face adversity with confidence. Now that's something to celebrate!

Depending on the message used, teachers can celebrate distinct areas of child development. When teachers are intentional about their use of positive messaging, they help families become more aware of their children's strengths and needs across cognitive, social-emotional, and behavioral domains. The following are some examples of positive message themes and the understanding they can provide to families during conferences.

- **Academic achievement:** Highlight student strengths in academic content areas. Identify specialized or advanced skills in individual topics of study. Parents of younger children may not follow grades and testing as closely as they do with older students, so sharing insight about cognitive growth is important.

- **Persistent effort/progress:** Steady and consistent effort leads to progress. Families need to know that, although their child may not have achieved a goal, they are moving in a positive direction. This information keeps families invested in supportive efforts.

- **Work habits:** Classroom rules and expectations make it possible for children to learn in a safe and structured setting. Complimenting work habits informs the family member of a child's level of maturity and sense of discipline. Strong work habits may also contribute to a child's growth mindset. Children with a well-developed growth mindset seek learning challenges and grow from their mistakes.

- **Metacognitive awareness:** Some students recognize how they learn best and apply this understanding to their learning choices in the classroom, which promotes success. This is a sophisticated skill that demonstrates students' focus and commitment to learning.

- **Relationship building:** Schools are social places. Relationship building in schools is crucial to productive interaction with peers and adults. Children who excel in demonstrating empathy and care for others are crucial to a collaborative learning community. Celebrating achievements in this area shares the value of classroom connections.

- **Self-regulation:** During the school day, children have to manage their emotions under many different circumstances. When families are aware of their children's advanced self-regulation, they can use it as a foundation for additional functional skills, such as risk-taking and time management.

- **Extracurricular activity:** Some children have enhanced skills in specialized areas of study. Experiences in drama, art, music, or athletics can expose students to newfound skill sets. Then, families can provide additional opportunities to develop these talents.

- **Leadership:** Even at a young age, children can show leadership expertise. Supporting peers and modeling appropriate behaviors are some simple illustrations of leadership skills in early childhood. When families know their children have these skills, they can support their development through age-appropriate responsibilities in the home.

Sharing positive messages with families can be easy and enjoyable. In the following scenario, Miss Diedre highlights Kimmi's willingness to work hard, learn from mistakes, and persevere—key elements of a growth mindset. This is a quality that some families may overlook among their children's strengths. Celebrating this talent helps teachers and families combine efforts to nurture this skill in the school and home setting.

Miss Diedre, a pre-K classroom teacher, waits anxiously for Mr. Won to arrive at his conference meeting. Miss Diedre has great news to share about Kimmi, Mr. Won's daughter.

When he arrives, Miss Diedre recounts the details of a recent observation with Kimmi. "The letter of the week is *R*," Miss Diedre explains. "Each day, the children will engage in a variety of interactive tasks to reinforce the letter shape and sound. Yesterday, in the art center, students were asked to draw a picture of rabbits."

"I see," said Mr. Won. "I know that was tricky for Kimmi. She tries so hard to make her drawings just right."

"Yes. It was a challenging task, but it is important for the children to try hard things," urged Miss Diedre.

"I agree," said Mr. Won. "So, how did Kimmi do?"

Miss Diedre shows Kimmi's work to Mr. Won. They both chuckle at the drawing. "See this first ear? Kimmi was unhappy with the shape, but instead of giving up, she made a few corrections. She then persisted with the task and drew the other ear. When she was ready to draw the body, Kimmi asked to borrow a picture book about rabbits to use as a model."

Mr. Won says with a smile, "Wow! I am so proud of her!"

"Yes, I am too." Miss Diedre adds, "And most importantly, Kimmi was proud of herself."

Teachers may need some practice with creating positive messaging. However, once they have trained their minds to see student strengths, developing positive messaging becomes much simpler. Moreover, teachers who learn to identify strengths readily often find it difficult to "unsee" students' capabilities. The following list offers some common examples of student behaviors that align with positive message themes.

- **Academic achievement:**
    - High test scores
    - Application of content skills

    - Advanced skill development
    - Effective writing skills
- **Persistent effort/progress:**
    - Consistent effort
    - Acceptance of failure as a learning opportunity
    - Gains in skill use
    - Ability to learn from mistakes
- **Work habits:**
    - Good listening skills
    - Neat student work
    - Organized workspace and materials
    - Compliant with directions
- **Metacognitive awareness:**
    - Understanding of learning needs
    - Self-selection and/or appropriate use of learning supports and resources
    - Self-awareness of skills
    - Acceptance of teacher support
- **Relationship building:**
    - Maintenance of peer relationships
    - Sense of empathy
    - Collaborative interactions
    - Appropriate negotiation of conflict
- **Self-regulation:**
    - Flexibility
    - Self-motivation
    - Stress-management skills
    - Focused attention
- **Extracurricular activity:**
    - Talents in sports, music, or the arts
    - Effective communication skills

- Good sense of humor
- Creativity

- **Leadership:**
    - Self-confidence
    - Sensible judgment
    - Emotional intelligence
    - Integrity

THEMES FOR POSITIVE MESSAGES FOR FAMILIES

Families have a significant influence on young students' success. At home, parents reinforce strong learning habits and nurture children's interests. Positive messages directed at families celebrate the efforts and sacrifices families make to help their children succeed. There is a very direct connection between family investment in home learning and student achievement. By celebrating family contributions, teachers highlight student progress as well. Consequently, family-positive messages offer teachers double the opportunity to begin the conference constructively. Teachers can use a variety of themes to celebrate family-school partnerships and to recognize family support:

- **Home learning support:** Many families will partner with teachers to reinforce academic, social, or behavioral goals in the home setting. Family-positive messages around home support provide feedback to families about the usefulness of their efforts.

- **Classroom engagement:** Teachers often provide many opportunities for families to participate in the classroom or school communities for or with their children. A simple acknowledgment of their time is a good way for teachers to motivate families to contribute again.

- **Collaboration:** Successful students have teachers and families that collaborate well. Showing appreciation to families that partner with teachers sustains positive relationship building.

- **Sharing insight:** Families and teachers have unique insights. While teachers have professional expertise in child development and instructional practice, families know their children best. Families that share their insight with teachers provide valuable information that supports effective teaching.

- **Support of decision-making:** In the classroom, teachers need to make difficult decisions. Having the support of families in making these tough choices builds teacher confidence and solidarity around efforts to support the student.

  Think of a child who frequently talks to peers during class. The teacher may decide to move his seat to a space in the front of the classroom to increase his attention and focus. This seating change may upset the child because he enjoys sitting with friends. Yet, when the teacher explains her reasoning for moving the child, the parent can show her support for the teacher's decision by helping the child to process the change. After first acknowledging the child's feelings, the parent may prompt the child to see this as an opportunity to improve his schoolwork and class participation.

At first, it may seem a little strange to focus on family positivity when the conference is about the child and their progress. As teachers know well, families play crucial roles in their children's success. Teachers who make time to celebrate families send a message that they value families as genuine thought partners in students' education. The following list provides some common examples of family behaviors that align with family-positive message themes.

- **Home learning support:**
  - Homework assistance/monitoring
  - Prioritizing school attendance
  - Practicing skills in the natural setting, such as reading print on a cereal box, counting tablespoons of sugar in a cooking recipe, and so on
- **Family engagement:**
  - Providing school supplies
  - Attending school events
  - Sharing career or talents with the classroom community
- **Collaboration:**
  - Returning forms/materials
  - Reinforcing goals
  - Resource sharing
- **Sharing insight:**
  - Offering student-specific data
  - Sharing student interests, preferences, and dislikes
  - Offering feedback on teacher recommendations

- **Support of decision-making:**
    - Supporting student consequences
    - Reinforcing classroom expectations
    - Soliciting teacher insight

How to Use the Positive Message Starter Tool

Positive messages are a simple way to begin the family conference productively. Teachers immediately get families on their side when they can share something specific and positive about their children. Further, when teachers celebrate student achievements, they are modeling effective ways to encourage and empower students and families. Parents learn how to identify their children's strengths and use them as a foundation for continued progress.

The Positive Message Starter Tool serves two distinctive purposes. First, the message starters can act as reflection prompts for identifying positive student behaviors and family supports. Second, the tool provides teachers with guidance to convert their thoughts on student progress into clear, cohesive, positive messages suitable for family-teacher conferencing. Teachers should note that personalization of these messages is necessary to create authenticity. Supplementing the suggested message starters with student names, specific behaviors, and practical evidence of progress demonstrates a genuine understanding of student strengths.

Family-teacher conferences are an ideal setting to celebrate students and families. Sharing positive messages with families sets an encouraging, hopeful tone for the conference. Further, noting a child's positive qualities underscores evidence of progress as well as potential assets for addressing challenges. Chapter 8 will discuss how teachers and families can incorporate that positive insight into effective planning for student success.

POSITIVE MESSAGE STARTER TOOL

Student Positive Message Starters:

"[Child's name] has made so much progress in . . ."

"I wish you could see how much [child's name] enjoys . . ."

"It makes me proud to see how [child's name] is learning to . . ."

"[Child's name] has a real talent for . . ."

"I am excited to share [child's name]'s growth in . . ."

"Let me show you some examples of [child's name]'s progress in . . ."

"I have a terrific story about your child . . ."

Family Positive Message Starters:

"I really appreciate your support with . . ."

"Thank you for reinforcing specific school expectations at home."

"I value your partnership with supporting [child's name] with . . ."

"You are such a strong model of specific skill for your child."

"I am grateful for your gift of time during [specific school event]."

"Your child is making such great progress because of your specific effort in the home. Thank you!"

CHAPTER 8

FOLLOWING UP AND FOLLOWING THROUGH

As a parent, I have to count on teachers to do what they say they're going to do. If they don't, we've all just wasted our time.

—PARENT OF A CHILD WITH A DISABILITY

As discussed in the previous chapters of this book, conducting effective family-teacher conferences is a complex process. From planning the conference to engaging families to problem-solving concerns, teachers must consider each aspect of the conference carefully and prepare accordingly. However, teacher responsibilities do not end when families exit the conference. Once teachers and families agree on strategies to support the child at home and school, both groups must execute their roles. At this time, the real conference work begins.

Responsive educators follow through with their obligations to the child and family. The parent quote at the beginning of the chapter illustrates the significant role responsiveness has in family-teacher conferences. Families cannot attend school with their children to oversee daily instruction and teacher interaction; they must rely on teachers to adhere to the plans discussed at the conference. When this commitment is broken, the family-teacher conference is far less effective for student progress.

On the other hand, teachers who are responsive to student needs send a clear message that they are invested and interested in student success. These teachers are concerned not just with building strong relationships with families during the conference but also with sustaining the relationship over time. Further, teacher responsiveness demonstrates appreciation for the family and their insight. This level of respect establishes the trust between teachers and families that lays the foundation for strong, collaborative partnerships.

Trust in the family-teacher relationship goes both ways. Effective action plans depend on student supports continuing in the home setting. Just as families depend on teachers to fulfill instructional obligations in the classroom, so too do teachers rely on families to follow through with their expected roles. When either the teacher or the family begins to disregard their responsibilities to the student, the momentum of progress may be lost. This is why accountability is so crucial to the integrity of the conferencing process.

By maintaining regular contact after the conference, teachers can reinforce and encourage family efforts. Through updates on students' growth and setbacks, teachers and families can work together to adjust or revise the action plan as needed. They can also celebrate student successes across school and home environments, increasing the child's support network. Positive trends in student progress affect teacher and family confidence levels, too. As families recognize the impact of their efforts, they grow more confident in their abilities to advocate for their children. Similarly, teachers become more assured in their interactions with families.

WHAT IS COMPASSIONATE RESPONDING?

When teachers cultivate a safe and welcoming conference environment, families may feel comfortable sharing personal concerns. While these apprehensions may relate directly to student needs, teachers who feel too deeply with families can develop their own social-emotional distress, called *secondary traumatic stress.*

Researchers Jennings and Min (2023) suggest compassionate responding as an alternative to an overabundance of empathy. Compassionate responding still uses care and concern to comfort individuals but also promotes a sense of self-reliance. The goal of compassionate responding is not to assume families' pain but to work with them to strengthen skill sets, such as self-reflection, persistence, self-awareness, and resourcefulness, that may lighten suffering.

Emotional self-regulation is a core element of compassionate responding. Teachers cannot console children and families to their own detriment. Taking time after conferencing to reflect on their own mental well-being is one of the best ways teachers can support families effectively.

After the Family-Teacher Conference

School conferences can be stressful for teachers. Also, planning and leading an effective conference takes concentrated effort and energy. It is no wonder that educators experience exhaustion and fatigue after conducting a series of conference meetings. Nonetheless, each family should receive the same level of energy and enthusiasm from the teacher when they come to the conference. The following strategies suggest ways teachers can sustain their professional investment both during the conference schedule and in the weeks to follow.

- **Decompress:** It is important that teachers take time directly after the conference to relax. Conferencing can place a great deal of tension and pressure on teachers. Engaging in mindfulness or self-care activities can help teachers to recover from a variety of social and emotional stressors.

- **Reflect:** Conferencing is a professional teaching responsibility. Much the same as planning or implementing lessons, teacher conferencing skills improve through thoughtful reflection and practice. Teachers should dedicate time to reflect on their conferencing skill strengths and needs within individual family meetings and across the conference schedule as a whole.

- **Organize notes:** Throughout the conference process, teachers should document family ideas, interests, and concerns appropriately. Organizing these notes after the conference can provide teachers with guidance for future interactions with families.

- **Complete follow-up tasks:** During conferencing, families may identify a need that requires outside assistance. For instance, a family may request information about a local after-school program or online resources on transitioning to kindergarten. Within the timeframe given in the conference, teachers should complete these tasks for families.

- **Thank families:** In most cases, attending school meetings is optional for families. As such, it is a kind gesture to thank families for participating in the conference. An email, card, or telephone call are all respectful ways to show appreciation for the family's time.

Connecting with Families Who Miss Conferences

At the end of conferencing, teachers should examine family participation rates. Although it may be tempting to criticize family members who do not attend, most would choose to join conference meetings if they could. Further, condemning families for missing a school conference does little to support the child. When teachers judge behaviors in this way, they risk isolating families from school activities permanently.

Instead, teachers should develop alternative means to connect with families who have missed conferences. In some cases, simply rescheduling the conference to a more convenient date and/or time may permit families to attend. If conferences were held in person, teachers might offer families a virtual or telephone option. Teachers might even consider forwarding a portfolio of student work for families to review, along with a two-way communication notebook for both parties to share thoughts and questions about student progress.

TIPS FOR CONNECTING WITH FAMILIES WHO MISS CONFERENCE MEETINGS

- Assume that families are eager and interested in attending their child's conference. If families do not attend, reach out to them to discuss options for rescheduling.
- Reflect on family needs. Consider what hindrance might have made it difficult for families to attend their scheduled conference. For future conference meetings, encourage school leadership to explore appropriate accommodations.
- Consider a home visit. If families are unable to come to the teacher, perhaps the teacher can come to the family. As an additional benefit, some families may feel more comfortable talking with teachers in their own homes or communities.
- Coordinate a conference meeting with a planned school visit for families. Try synchronizing meetings with student arrival or departure times or special school events, such as an open house, art show, school play, and so on.
- Assign students a central role in the conference meeting. Young children can share their school interests or preferences, and older children can discuss school goals, activities, or upcoming projects. Be sure families know that the children have prepared to lead the conference. Encourage families to attend conferences to see their children discuss their progress.

Developing a Post-Conference Action Plan

Teachers and families can implement an action plan after the conference to make sure children succeed. The major purpose of an action plan is to identify the specific individual steps needed to meet an identified student's goals. A written record of goals and behaviors holds all stakeholders accountable as well. Having this level of organization prevents loss of learning time by making efficient use of efforts and resources. Further, well-designed action plans set an appropriate timeframe for meeting goals as well as a system for collecting data on student progress.

With each of its functional elements, the conference action plan provides many benefits to teachers and families. First, the action plan should document the major discussion points in the conference. Setting actionable goals and assigned roles underscores a path forward as teachers and families collaborate to address student concerns. Second, the action plan creates a timeline for meeting learning targets. With this knowledge easily accessible, teachers and families can stay invested in student progress over time. Third, the action plan documents student progress toward goals. Monitoring data in this way allows teachers to adjust the plan as needed rather than waiting until the end of the grading period. The following list names and defines each element of the conference action plan.

- **Student goal:** the expected outcome and how meeting this objective supports student growth and development
- **Action steps:** prioritize tasks that members of the team will fulfill to meet the identified goal
- **Participant roles:** defines specific action areas for family, teachers, school leadership, and the student
- **Completion timeline:** an appropriate timeframe for completing or revisiting the student goal. In some cases, the team may need to set timelines to meet smaller goals before addressing the most significant issue.
- **Progress monitoring system:** how the team will verify when the student goal is met. Data monitoring should identify who will collect data, how often, and through what measures.

SETTING STUDENT GOALS

Goal setting is fundamental to student achievement. Consequently, teachers and families must think carefully as they identify student outcomes. Working toward useful and appropriate goals supports learning important skill sets, including time management, progress monitoring, cognitive flexibility, and metacognitive awareness. As these skills apply to many thinking activities, mastering them places students on a pathway to independent growth and development.

Teachers, families, and children should set action plan goals with thoughtful intention. First proposed by George Doran in 1981, SMART goals are defined as specific, measurable, achievable, relevant, and timebound. Goals are specific when they are tangible and measurable and when there is a way to track progress. Achievable goals strike a balance between being attainable and challenging, while relevant goals align with long-term expectations for student learning. Lastly, timebound goals have a timeframe for completion. Teachers and families should consider each of these criteria when identifying action plan goals.

ACTION STEPS AND PARTICIPANT ROLES

Once the goals are set, teachers will need to think about the action steps that make realizing the goal possible. Action steps should consider all the activities that teachers and families need to do to equip the student for success. For

SAMPLE ACTION PLAN SMART GOAL

Student goal: In three of five daily center rotations, the child will share toys with at least two peers without teacher intervention.

- **Specific:** The goal outlines a specific activity for the child. She will share toys with a peer independently.
- **Measurable:** The goal is measurable. The teacher can observe the child and count sharing exchanges.
- **Achievable:** Meeting this goal with 60 percent accuracy (three out of five center rotations) is a good starting point for a young student who struggles with sharing independently. As the child's sharing skills improve, the teacher can easily adjust this benchmark.
- **Relevant:** Sharing is a critical social skill for young children. Those who share easily will connect better with peers.
- **Timebound:** The teacher can track this goal daily during center rotations.

instance, the teacher may need specialized resources or materials. Families may need to organize their schedules to accommodate tutoring sessions. Teachers should review action plans to ensure they are prioritized appropriately. In this way, the overarching goal of the action plan is organized into manageable tasks that give the student the best opportunity to be successful.

Action steps should be directly assigned to the action plan participants. At a minimum, the teacher, family, and child should each have participant roles. It is also sometimes useful to include other members of the child's support network. Participant roles share accountability among all members of the team. Specifically, determining the frequency for each action step will sustain focus and motivation for the action plan. Assigning roles to adults at school and at home also sends a message to students that their teachers and families are unified in their expectations.

SAMPLE ACTION STEPS AND PARTICIPANT ROLES

Student goal: In three of five daily center rotations, the student will share toys with at least two peers without teacher intervention.

Action Steps	Responsible Participants	Frequency
• Discuss the purpose of sharing. • Define what sharing looks like in a variety of settings.	• Classroom teacher • Family	When demonstrating inappropriate behavior
• Set expectations for sharing. Discuss rewards and consequences in the home and school.	• Classroom teacher • Family • Child	When demonstrating inappropriate behavior
Model sharing strategies with the student.	• Classroom teacher • Family • Child • Peers	Daily
Read age-appropriate children's literature with sharing themes.	• Classroom teacher • Family • Student	Weekly
Prepare an observation sheet to track data in school.	Classroom teacher	Review weekly
Collect student data.	Classroom teacher	Daily
Identify a daily system of sharing data with the family.	Classroom teacher	Review weekly
Review progress with student.	• Family • Student	Daily

MONITORING AND REVISITING THE ACTION PLAN

There are many ways that teachers can monitor student progress toward a goal. Monitoring progress in the action plan documents student progress for all stakeholders. Depending on the goal set, teachers may choose to use observational records, frequency charts, student work, or video/audio recordings. The data teachers collect from these records can then be shared with students and families. This information assists the teacher and family in making informed decisions about revisions to the action plan. Sharing progress with the child also builds ownership in the intervention process, creating self-awareness and confidence in skills.

The teacher and family should agree on when to revisit the action plan. Some goals may require the team to discuss progress at regular intervals, such as weekly, while other plans may only need to be adjusted as students meet goals or encounter problems. Nevertheless, it is always useful to connect with the family within the first week of implementing the action plan to discuss general feedback on action steps and/or to supply support and resources for the home setting. At this first review meeting, the teacher and family may set an interval for reviewing the action plan in the future as well as an expected timeframe for goal completion.

How to Use the Conference Action Plan Template Tool

Creating an action plan is a useful way for teachers and families to translate student goals into actionable steps. While the conference setting is ideal for discussing overarching goals and participant roles, teachers will need to dedicate time after the conference for outlining the specific plan details. This arrangement provides both teachers and families with time to reflect on how to best support the student through their efforts, time, and resources.

When the teacher has completed the action plan, she can share it with families for initial feedback. Certainly, teachers will want to share a complete and organized draft of the plan with families, but the aim is not perfection. There will always be areas of improvement and revision for the team to consider. After all, it is difficult to evaluate the action plan fully until the teacher has put it in place. As such, it is important for teachers to implement the action plan and to begin gathering data as soon as possible.

The Conference Action Plan Template Tool offers a guide for designing an action plan for student success. The template gives teachers a place to document ideas and strategies for reaching student goals. The document also includes a place to identify scheduled times when teachers and families will revisit and revise the action plan. Teachers can make note of parent feedback or changes to the action plan and set an expected date of completion. As a whole, the action plan serves as a visual representation of the team's commitment to student success.

What happens after the family-teacher conference is as important as what occurs during the meeting. Long after the close of the conference, teachers must continue to work with families to establish a useful action plan for student success. Such teacher accountability, along with the other critical strategies discussed in this book, sets the stage for positive family-teacher interaction. In this way, the conference can transform into a stable foundation for long-term student achievement.

CONFERENCE ACTION PLAN TEMPLATE TOOL

Student Goal*: ____

____

Action Steps	Responsible Participants	Frequency

*Student goals should follow SMART (specific, measurable, achievable, relevant, timebound) criteria.

Progress Monitoring System**

Tool Used	Area of Growth	Collection Schedule	Data Collector

**Attach a copy of the observational tool that will be used for progress monitoring.

Revisiting Schedule

Inital Review	Feedback & Revision Notes
Date ______________ □ In-Person □ Phone □ Virtual	

Review #2	Feedback & Revision Notes
Date ______________________ □ In-Person □ Phone □ Virtual	

Review #3	Feedback & Revision Notes
Date ______________________ □ In-Person □ Phone □ Virtual	

Final Review	Feedback & Revision Notes
Date ______________________ □ In-Person □ Phone □ Virtual	

Teacher Signature ____

Family Signature ____

Appendices

Appendix A: Family Questionnaire

Appendix B: Family-Teacher Conference Planning Tool

Appendix C: Welcoming Classroom Teacher Checklist

Appendix D: Effective Conference Communication Practicing Tool

Appendix E: Family-Teacher Conference Documentation Gathering Tool

Appendix F: Problem Solving through Choice Reflection Tool

Appendix G: Positive Message Starter Tool

Appendix H: Conference Action Plan Template Tool

FAMILY QUESTIONNAIRE

Welcome to our classroom! I am excited to work with you to make this a positive school year for your child. Please complete this questionnaire so that I can learn a little more about your family's interests, talents, and traditions.

Child's name:

Family member's name: **Relationship to the child:**

Family Information:

Who lives at home with the child? Please include names and relationships.

Does your family have any pets? If so, what kind?

Family Interests:

How does your family spend time together?

Briefly describe a recent or memorable family vacation or special outing.

Family Traditions:

What holidays/special days does your family celebrate?

What special traditions does your family have for these days?

Additional Information:

Is there anything else you would like to share about your family?

FAMILY-TEACHER CONFERENCE PLANNING TOOL

Student Name:

Family Attending:

Conference Date:

Faculty/Staff Attending:

Conference Purpose:

Special Family Needs (check all that apply):

- ☐ Individualized Conference Scheduling
- ☐ Language Interpreter
- ☐ Additional Time
- ☐ Virtual/Phone Setting
- ☐ Supplemental Attendees
- ☐ Other____________________

Conference Goals

Teacher-Directed Goals

Family-Directed Goals

Positive Student Notes

Academic

Behavioral

Social

Student Concerns

Concerns

Classroom Documentation

Family Questions

1. ______________________________

2. ______________________________

3. ______________________________

WELCOMING CLASSROOM TEACHER CHECKLIST

One Month Before the Conference

- ☐ Connect with each family via phone or in person at a school event.
- ☐ Provide opportunities for families to self-select conference meeting times.
- ☐ Explore technology platform options for virtual conferences.
- ☐ Learn the correct pronunciation of family names.
- ☐ Appraise the classroom decor, resources, and design for inclusive messaging and representation.

One Week Before the Conference

- ☐ Tidy the meeting environment.
- ☐ Secure appropriate seating options.
- ☐ Test virtual meeting platforms and equipment.
- ☐ Create a comfortable and engaging waiting space for families who arrive early.
- ☐ Forward personalized conference reminders (printed or digital) that underscore enthusiasm for meeting with families.

The Day of the Conference

- ☐ Demonstrate a friendly and welcoming disposition.
- ☐ Meet families at the classroom door.
- ☐ Greet each family by name.
- ☐ Escort families to the meeting space. Offer seating to all participants.
- ☐ Begin the conference with pleasantries that show care and concern for the family's well-being.

APPENDIX D: EFFECTIVE CONFERENCE COMMUNICATION PRACTICING TOOL

EFFECTIVE CONFERENCE COMMUNICATION PRACTICING TOOL

1. Using an Assertive Communication Style

For many families, teachers serve as a resource for understanding developmentally appropriate and grade-level expectations. Teacher expertise in child development and instructional practice, coupled with child-specific knowledge, helps families make informed decisions. Also, an assertive communication style supports families' confidence in teacher knowledge and skills. How could a teacher employ an assertive teaching style in this situation?

> Kristina has been struggling in your first-grade class. With intensive, one-on-one teaching, Kristina can now recognize all letters and most letter sounds. Despite this progress, you are still concerned that Kristina will not meet grade-level standards by the close of the school year, and you believe retention is necessary.

Notes:

2. Asking Open-Ended Questions

Open-ended questions encourage families to elaborate on their ideas and thoughts. Pointed questions can clarify understanding and illuminate the underlying issue. How might open-ended questions highlight the driving force behind this parent's concern?

> Jakob is a student in your pre-K classroom. Recently, Jakob's father has scheduled a conference with you. When he arrives, he is visibly upset. "Jakob comes home crying every day," he begins the conversation. "Why don't you like my son?"

Notes:

3. Confirming Understanding

Asking questions, paraphrasing ideas, and summarizing central themes are all useful ways teachers can confirm family messaging in the conference setting. Taking time to verify what is said maintains the integrity of the conference. In what ways might a teacher confirm understanding in these circumstances?

> Rashawn is a new student in your second-grade classroom. His mother is concerned about his transition to the new district. During the conference, she mentions that he does not talk about friends, complains of being "bored" at recess, and now is reluctant to go to school.

Notes:

APPENDIX E: FAMILY-TEACHER CONFERENCE DOCUMENTATION GATHERING TOOL

FAMILY-TEACHER CONFERENCE DOCUMENTATION GATHERING TOOL

Student Name: ______________________ **Conference Date:** ____________

Student Strengths

____

____

Student Growth: Documentation Prepared

- ☐ Student Work/Projects
- ☐ Photos
- ☐ Assessments
- ☐ Tests
- ☐ Video/Audio
- ☐ Checklists
- ☐ Frequency Charts
- ☐ Interviews
- ☐ Portfolios

Notes:

Student Challenges

____

____

Student Concerns: Documentation Prepared

- ☐ Student Work/Projects
- ☐ Photos
- ☐ Assessments
- ☐ Tests
- ☐ Video/Audio
- ☐ Checklists
- ☐ Frequency Charts
- ☐ Interviews
- ☐ Portfolios

Notes:

Key Insights from Documentation

Questions and Follow-Up Concerns

APPENDIX F: PROBLEM SOLVING THROUGH CHOICE REFLECTION TOOL

PROBLEM SOLVING THROUGH CHOICE REFLECTION TOOL

Example scenario:

Family: "I don't want my child enrolled in the math readiness program."

Teacher: "The math readiness program provides intensive, small-group reinforcement of foundational number skills. However, working one-on-one with your child at home, seeking an outside tutoring service, and continuing our current classroom supports are all good options, too. As the child's parent, you know his capabilities best."

Practice scenario: Add choices

Family: "There's no way I can find the time to read to my child every night."

Teacher: "Reading at home builds literacy skills and strengthens vocabulary development, but at present, it is not a required home-learning assignment."

What choices might the teacher provide for this family with respect to this concern?

____

____

____

Practice scenario: Add the teacher's perspective

Family: "I don't want my daughter to take a nap in kindergarten."

Teacher: "Students can recharge for the afternoon in many ways. Would you prefer to have your child read books quietly or listen to music with headphones during rest time?"

What might be the teacher's perspective on this family concern?

____

____

____

Teacher-suggested scenario

What family opinion might be brought up at the next school conference? How will you stress your perspective but provide the family with reasonable options for meeting the child's needs?

Family: ____

____

Teacher: ____

____

____

POSITIVE MESSAGE STARTER TOOL

Student Positive Message Starters:

"[Child's name] has made so much progress in . . ."

"I wish you could see how much [child's name] enjoys . . ."

"It makes me proud to see how [child's name] is learning to . . ."

"[Child's name] has a real talent for . . ."

"I am excited to share [child's name]'s growth in . . ."

"Let me show you some examples of [child's name]'s progress in . . ."

"I have a terrific story about your child . . ."

Family Positive Message Starters:

"I really appreciate your support with . . ."

"Thank you for reinforcing specific school expectations at home."

"I value your partnership with supporting [child's name] with . . ."

"You are such a strong model of specific skill for your child."

"I am grateful for your gift of time during [specific school event]."

"Your child is making such great progress because of your specific effort in the home. Thank you!"

APPENDIX H: CONFERENCE ACTION PLAN TEMPLATE TOOL

CONFERENCE ACTION PLAN TEMPLATE TOOL

Student Goal*: ____

____

Action Steps	Responsible Participants	Frequency

*Student goals should follow SMART (specific, measurable, achievable, relevant, timebound) criteria.

Progress Monitoring System**

Tool Used	Area of Growth	Collection Schedule	Data Collector

**Attach a copy of the observational tool that will be used for progress monitoring.

Revisiting Schedule

Inital Review	Feedback & Revision Notes
Date ______________________ ☐ In-Person ☐ Phone ☐ Virtual	

Review #2	Feedback & Revision Notes
Date ______________________ ☐ In-Person ☐ Phone ☐ Virtual	

Review #3	Feedback & Revision Notes
Date ______________________ ☐ In-Person ☐ Phone ☐ Virtual	

Final Review	Feedback & Revision Notes
Date ______________________ ☐ In-Person ☐ Phone ☐ Virtual	

Teacher Signature ____

Family Signature ____

References and Additional Resources

Bredekamp, Sue. 2019. *Effective Practices in Early Childhood Education: Building a Foundation.* 4th ed. London, UK: Pearson.

Brittingham Furlonge, Nicole. 2020. "'Apprentices of Listening': Sound Studies in Educational Leadership." *English Studies in Canada* 46(2): 303-306. https://doi.org/10.1353/esc.2020.a903563

Centers for Disease Control and Prevention. 2023. "Data and Statistics on Children's Mental Health." Centers for Disease Control and Prevention. https://www.cdc.gov/childrensmentalhealth/data.html

Doran, George T. 1981. "There's a S.M.A.R.T. Way to Write Management's Goals and Objectives." *Journal of Management Review* 70: 35-36.

Dweck, Carol S. 2006. *Mindset: The New Psychology of Success.* New York: Random House.

EDIT.org. n.d. "Free Printable Parent-Teacher Conference Forms." https://edit.org/blog/teacher-parent-conference-templates

Epstein, Joyce L., Mavis G. Sanders, and Steven Sheldon. 2019. *School, Family, and Community Partnerships: Your Handbook for Action*. 4th ed. Thousand Oaks, CA: Corwin.

Ferlazzo, Larry. 2011. "Involvement or Engagement?" *Educational Leadership* 68(8): 10-14.

Genta, Monica. 2023. "How to Have the Most Effective Teacher Conferences of Your Career (and It's a Super Simple Structure)." September 17. *This Teacher Life* [Audio podcast]. https://podcasts.apple.com/us/podcast/this-teacher-life/id1477926278?i=1000628180189

González, Norma, Luis C. Moll, and Cathy Amanti. 2005. *Funds of Knowledge: Theorizing Practices in Households, Communities, and Classrooms*. Mahwah, NJ: Lawrence Erlbaum Associates.

Harvard Family Research Project. 2010. *Parent-Teacher Conference Tip Sheets for Principals, Teachers, and Parents*. Cambridge, MA: Harvard Graduate School of Education.

Harvard Family Research Project. 2013. *Tips for Administrators, Teachers, and Families: How to Share Data Effectively*. Cambridge, MA: Harvard Graduate School of Education.

Henderson, Anne T., Vivian Johnson, Karen L. Mapp, and Don Davies. 2007. *Beyond the Bake Sale: The Essential Guide to Family-School Partnerships*. New York: The New Press.

Jennings, Patricia A., and Helen H. Min. 2023. "Transforming Empathy-Based Stress to Compassion: Skillful Means to Preventing Teacher Burnout." *Mindfulness* 14(10): 2311–2322. https://doi.org/10.1007/s12671-023-02115-6

Katz, Neil, and Kevin McNulty. 1994. *Reflective Listening*. https://www.maxwell.syr.edu/docs/default-source/ektron-files/reflective-listening-neil-katz-and-kevin-mcnulty.pdf?sfvrsn=f1fa6672_7

Muhs, Mary. 2018. *Family Engagement in Early Childhood Settings*. St. Paul, MN: Redleaf Press.

National Association for the Education of Young Children. n.d. *Principles of Effective Family Engagement*. https://www.naeyc.org/resources/topics/family-engagement/principles

National Association for the Education of Young Children. 2019. "Definitions of Key Terms." Advancing Equity in Early Childhood Education Position Statement. https://www.naeyc.org/resources/position-statements/equity/definitions

National Center for Educational Statistics. 2024. "English Learners in Public Schools." https://nces.ed.gov/programs/coe/indicator/cgf/english-learners

National Clearinghouse for English Language Acquisition. 2024. https://ncela.ed.gov

Seitz, Hilary. 2008. "The Power of Documentation in the Early Childhood Classroom." *Young Children* 63(2): 88–93.

Skoog-Hoffman, Ally, et al. 2023. *Building Authentic School-Family Partnerships through the Lens of Social and Emotional Learning*. Chicago, IL: Collaborative for Academic and Social Emotional Learning. https://casel.org/sel-innovations-1/?download=true

Teachers Pay Teachers. 2024. Free conference form. https://www.teacherspayteachers.com/browse?search=free%20conference%20form

Tervalon, Melanie, and Jann Murray-García, J. 1998. "Cultural Humility versus Cultural Competence: A Critical Distinction in Defining Physician Training Outcomes in Multicultural Education." *Journal of Health Care for the Poor and Underserved* 9(2): 117–125.

Vaughn, Lisa M., Janet R. Forbes, and Britteny Howell. 2009. "Enhancing Home Visitation Programs: Input from a Participatory Evaluation Using Photovoice."

Infants & Young Children: An Interdisciplinary Journal of Early Childhood Intervention 22(2): 132–145.

Wang, Caroline, and Mary Ann Burris. 1997. "Photovoice: Concept, Methodology, and Use for Participatory Needs Assessment." *Health Education & Behavior* 24(3): 369–387.

Young, Wendy, and Paige DeLozier. 2023. "Propelling Progress Post-Conference: How to Drive Momentum with Families" [webinar]. October 24. EdWeb. https://home.edweb.net/webinar/engagement20231024/

Index

F

R

S

T

V

W